No Saints, No Saviors

Best Regards,

Willie DeKine

2006

No Saints,

No Saviors

My Years with

The Allman Brothers Band

By

Willie Perkins

MERCER UNIVERSITY PRESS
Macon, Georgia
25th Anniversary

ISBN 0-86554-967-2
MUP/H688

© 2005 Mercer University Press
1400 Coleman Avenue
Macon, Georgia 31207
All rights reserved

Second Printing

∞The paper used in this publication meets the minimum
requirements of American National Standard for Information
Sciences—Permanence of Paper for Printed Library Materials,
ANSI Z39.48-1992.

Library of Congress Cataloging-in-Publication Data

CIP data are available from the Library of Congress

Contents

vi

For My Loving Mother

and

Elizabeth;

Rest in Peace

Duane Allman, Berry Oakley, Twiggs Lyndon,

Lamar Williams, Joe Dan Petty, Allen Woody,

Buffalo Evans

Foreword

In December 1969, I was seated sixth row left to see Blood, Sweat, & Tears headline at the Fillmore East. According to the concert program (which I still have), one of the opening acts was The Allman Brothers Band. I'd never heard of them, but I remember how they looked and what they sounded like—almost exactly.

A thin, good-looking, long-haired blond guy sat behind a big Hammond organ and sang his heart out like an aging black blues man who had actually suffered the blues before he got around to singing about them. He was Gregg Allman.

Standing next to him was an orange-haired boy with skinny legs and walrus chops playing the slide guitar. He stood there with his eyes closed while his guitar spoke to me. I was riveted. It cried. It soared. I couldn't believe my ears. I'd never heard anyone play that way before, and I haven't since. I was awestruck. He made me shiver. He was Duane Allman.

A dark-haired guitarist stood to his left, easing out sweet yet sharp licks that wove and wound themselves around Duane's melodies. There were times when he'd step forward, eyes closed, bent backwards, taking the lead, his guitar singing. He was Dickey Betts.

And then there was the bass player, also skinny, in a tattered tank top and ripped jeans, his bass slung low, his sweaty long hair tucked behind his ears, pumping his legs rhythmically. His playing was so mesmerizing, deep down, and low that I could feel the notes in the pit of my stomach. He was Berry Oakley.

The drummers were perfectly in synch with each other, their intricate rhythms keeping it all together. They were Butch Trucks and Jai Johanny Johanson, aka Jaimoe.

For the next two years, I bought the group's albums and attended their shows as much as I could. I researched their roots and influences and discovered Bobby Blue Bland, T Bone Walker, and Robert Johnson, among many others. I bought all of Duane's session work with people like Aretha Franklin, Wilson Pickett, and John Hammond, Jr.

When "Layla" was released and touted as Eric Clapton's masterpiece, I knew Duane was the one making many of those magical sounds. And "Layla" played on my turntable when, by chance on a Saturday afternoon, I read that Duane had been killed in a motorcycle accident. I was crushed.

But the band persevered and so did I. In 1971, a friend and I traveled to Providence, Rhode Island, for a concert. It was there that I met Willie Perkins. Not coincidentally, my friend and I stayed in the same hotel as the band and their crew. I wanted to get close to the music that had become so important to me, and after some creative logistics I managed to secure a spot backstage. One of my most memorable experiences began when Red Dog offered me a seat—an equipment case he pushed close to Berry's spot on stage. At some point mid-show, Berry spilled a can of beer all over me. He looked terribly concerned and kept glancing at me apologetically throughout the rest of the show. It didn't matter to me. I felt like I'd been baptized.

For the next three years, Willie and I saw each other whenever we could, mostly when the band was working in the northeast. We exchanged letters. Mine were lengthy and detailed. His were short and sweet. He was a busy man. We lost touch around 1974 but reconnected via the Internet a few years ago. He has always been and will always be one of the most important people in my life.

This is his story.

Elizabeth LaGrua
New York City
July 2004

Acknowledgments

This is not a definitive history of The Allman Brothers Band. It is a personal memoir of my years with the band and with Gregg Allman's solo band from 1970 to 1989. Specific performance dates, earnings, album recording and release dates, and contractual terms come from my personal records retained over the years. I also refer to old tour programs that I originally helped prepare as well as old magazine and newspaper articles.

I want to thank the following people for granting me interviews and for their kind support and assistance: Chuck and Rose Lane Leavell, Scott Hayes, Charles Bignon, Phil Walden, Donna Allman, John Condon, Joe Sedita, Red Dog, Kim Payne, Gerald "Buffalo" Evans, Alex Hodges, Randy Short, A. J. Lyndon, "Scoots" Lyndon, and John "Scooter" Herring. I would also like to thank the photographers who generously contributed their work to this book. A special thanks goes to Kirk West for his support and help and for the hours he spent going through The Allman Brothers Band photo archives with my photo editor and me.

I thank Gus Arrendale for his early support, without which this project would never have gotten started, and Elizabeth LaGrua for her brilliant photo editing, her painstaking transcription of my handwritten manuscript, her ideas and recollections, and her loving support and encouragement.

Finally, thanks to Marc Jolley and the staff at Mercer University Press for believing in me and in the story I wanted to tell.

Macon Coliseum, Macon, GA, 1971   © *W. Robert Johnson*

The band on the steps of the house where the cover of the first album was taken.
Macon, GA, 1969. ©Twiggs Lyndon

Author Willie Perkins with money bag and briefcase, backstage at a gig, 1971
©*Suzanne Lukas Terven*

Twiggs Lyndon, mid 1970's

Duane Allman backstage in the dressing room of the Warehouse, New Orleans, Fall 1971. It was his last performance in New Orleans
©*Sidney Smith/www.rockstarphotos.net*

Berry Oakley after a gig in a hotel room, Fall 1972 shortly before his death
©Sidney Smith/www.rockstarphotos.net

Gregg Allman at the farm, Juliette, GA, 1973   ©*Sidney Smith/www.rockstarphotos.net*

(l-r) **Red Dog, Tuffy Phillips and Twiggs Lyndon at the farm, Juliette, GA**
©*Sidney Smith/www.rockstarphotos.net*

(l-r) **Kim Payne, Dickey Betts, Buffalo Evans and Tuffy Phillips at the farm,
Juliette, GA**   ©*Sidney Smith/www.rockstarphotos.net*

(From top left to center) **At the band office, Macon, GA, mid 1970's:**
Earl "Speedo" Simms, Scott Hayes, Hewell "Chank" Middleton, Charles Bignon,
John "Scooter" Herring

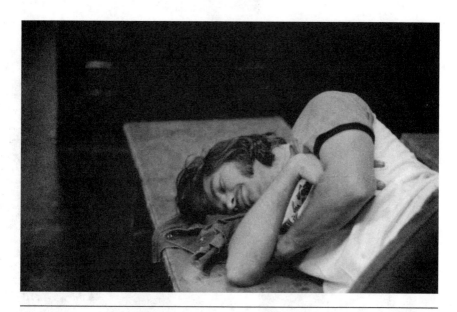

Mike Callahan asleep backstage at a gig, early 1970's
©Kathy Winner/courtesy Randy Short

Joe Dan Petty with Dickey Betts backstage at the Cow Palace in San Francisco, 1973-74
©Sidney Smith/www.rockstarphotos.net

Macon Coliseum, Macon, GA 1971   ©W. Robert Johnson

Phil Walden with Bill Graham at the annual Capricorn picnic, Macon, GA, 1974
©Sidney Smith/www.rockstarphotos.net

Phil Walden with former President Jimmy Carter, then Georgia's governor, at the
Capricorn offices, Macon, GA, late 1973   *©Sidney Smith/www.rockstarphotos.net*

1

First Day on the Job

It was late May 1970, the beginning of another hot and humid summer in Macon, Georgia. Days earlier, I had been a short-haired, coat-and-tie-wearing auditor for the Trust Company of Georgia in Atlanta, the bank of the Coca-Cola millionaires whose hallowed vaults contain the exact combination of ingredients for the secret soft drink formula.

Today, I had a new job as road manager for The Allman Brothers Band, a virtually unknown rock band from the South that courted a small but growing cult following. As I made my way up the walkway at 2321 Vineville Avenue, I realized I was about to embark on a great adventure. This was the "Big House," the rented home of Duane Allman, Gregg Allman, and Berry Oakley and the official band headquarters. It would also become my home for the next several months. I was to take up residency on one of the couches in the first floor living room while my girlfriend, Sandra Hinkle, modeled in Atlanta and kept our apartment there.

At the time, nobody was home but Joan Roosman, the younger sister of Duane's wife Donna. Joan cordially introduced herself, showed me around the house, and offered me iced tea. There were two iced tea containers in the fridge, one marked with gray duct tape. Joan warned me not to drink from the duct-taped container unless I didn't have anything planned for the next twenty-four to forty-eight hours as it was laced with LSD and highly electric. Yes, this indeed was the beginning of a great adventure. How in the world had I gotten here?

2

Beginnings

I was born April 18, 1940, in Augusta, Georgia, the son of Addie Bentley Perkins and William Hardwick Perkins. I had an older sister, Harriette, and later a younger brother, Charles. From my birth until I turned five, our family lived in various army base towns as my father had enlisted and became a captain in the infantry. He subsequently died in January 1945 from wounds received in the Battle of the Bulge, Hitler's last great offensive.

In 1958, I was a senior in high school at Richmond Academy in Augusta, a public military school where ROTC was mandatory. My dad had been a cadet lieutenant colonel of the school battalion, but I was a lowly buck sergeant squad leader. I only got that rank because I set up my company commander with a hot blonde he had wanted to date. I was constantly getting demerits for "long hair," which must have been all of two inches, and a "dirty rifle." I tried to be a good soldier, but military life was not for me. My interests ran more in the areas of fast cars, faster women, and black music. My musical credo was "If it's white, it ain't right."

Augusta was a good R&B radio town, but radio really starting rocking after dark. That's when *red-blooded* boys from all over the South tuned in to 1510 on the AM dial. "WLAC, Nashville, Tennessee...the 50,000-watt broadcast service of the Life and Casualty Insurance Company." Top deejays were John R., Gene Nobles, and the "Jivin' Hoss Man." Every night, their clear channel signal blasted Chuck Berry, Little Richard, Bo Diddley, Muddy Waters, The Howling Wolf, and countless others all over the Southeast. Some nights, I could even hear the maniacal Wolfman Jack from Del Rio, Texas, on the border with Mexico. If you've never heard the Wolfman do a commercial for "100 live baby chicks, just $3.98," you haven't truly lived. "Now, just imagine all the fun you're gonna have with these baby chicks. You lead 'em around on little leashes, you give 'em little names, and then when they grow up—you gonna eat 'em!" (Wolfman, from *Border Radio*, Gene Fowler and Bill Crawford, Texas Monthly Press, Austin, Texas, 1987).

During my senior year at Richmond Academy, I began noticing a new kid in town. His name was Scott Hayes and he drove a pretty neat '48 Plymouth coupe. We started talking cars and music and discovered we had a lot in common. It turns out that he was from Macon, Georgia, and in the vernacular of the day, he and his girlfriend "had to get married." They both got kicked out of school and were living with Scott's brother in Augusta while Scott finished school and his new wife Patricia had their first son. Scott and I have remained close friends for more than forty years. Like me, he would eventually work for The Allman Brothers Band. First, though, Scott introduced me to Twiggs.

3

Twiggs

After graduation, Scott moved back to Macon to attend Mercer University. I briefly attended Georgia Tech, then transferred to the University of Georgia in Athens. Our paths didn't cross much again until speed week at Daytona Beach in 1962. During this period in the early sixties, I first met Twiggs through Scott Hayes.

Twiggs Miller Lyndon, Jr., better known as Twiggs, was a unique individual—an absolute perfectionist living in an absolutely imperfect world. He was born in Macon on October 26, 1942, and grew up there. The story goes that he was due to graduate high school in 1960, but he came up one credit short. Rather than simply taking the one course, he insisted on taking the entire curriculum over again, plus ROTC, in which he organized a crack precision drill team. After graduating, Twiggs joined the navy and later ended up going AWOL. Scott Hayes and I sheltered him for a while and eventually talked him into turning himself in, but he somehow beat the rap. He then ran afoul of the navy again by growing a beard and refusing to cut it off. He was able to overcome this problem by finding an obscure naval regulation that apparently allowed for a beard. By this time, though, Twiggs and the navy had had enough of each other, and he was given a discharge.

In summer 1964, Twiggs, Scott Hayes, and I took a road trip that ended up in Las Vegas. Before driving nonstop back to Macon, Scott and I dropped Twiggs off at the Vegas Greyhound terminal. With seven dollars plus change and some World War II surplus C-rations for food, he headed toward Los Angeles on a whim. While there, he encountered and introduced himself to another Macon native, Richard Penniman, better known as Little Richard. Twiggs ended up serving a couple of stints as Little Richard's road manager. At one point, he hired a young guitar player away from Jackie Wilson's band in front of the Royal Peacock Supper Club in Atlanta. That guitar player was a youngster named Jimi Hendrix. Some claim Hendrix picked up a few guitar licks from Macon's legendary blues legend, Johnny Jenkins, when Twiggs introduced the two.

Twiggs eventually left Little Richard for good, and after various odd jobs, Phil Walden Artists and Promotions back in Macon hired him. Phil and his younger brother Alan owned the Walden office. At the time, it was the premier R&B and soul music agency and management company. Otis Redding was their number-one client. At one time or another, Twiggs was associated with Sam and Dave, Johnny Jenkins, Percy Sledge, Johnny Taylor, and Arthur Conley. He became adept at working with difficult artists and promoters. In those days, it was not unheard of for the club owner who just paid an artist inside to attempt to rob him at gunpoint outside in the parking lot—that is, if the artist was slick enough to get paid all or part of the money he was owed in the first place.

By fall 1968, there was a huge buzz about a phenomenal guitarist named Duane Allman who had signed on as a session player for producer Rick Hall at the Fame Recording Studios in Muscle Shoals, Alabama. His work had caught the ears of Jerry Wexler of Atlantic Records and of Phil Walden. Eventually, Phil bought Duane's contract from Rick Hall and planned to form a band around Duane for Walden's new Capricorn record label to be distributed by Atlantic. Walden sent Twiggs and Jai Johnny Johanson—aka "Jaimoe," who had been a drummer with Otis Redding and others—to Muscle Shoals. Duane later asked Jaimoe to be in his new band, and Twiggs was their first road manager.

The story of the formation of The Allman Brothers Band has been told many times, and I won't retell it here. Suffice it to say that by early 1969, the band was playing gigs while Duane continued to perform in many Atlantic sessions with Wilson Pickett, Aretha Franklin, Clarence Carter, King Curtis, and others. Twiggs kept telling me about Duane and the new band. Finally, in spring 1969, I saw and heard them at Piedmont Park in Atlanta for the first time. I had never heard anything like them in my life, and more than thirty years later, I still have not heard anything that matches the emotion, the excitement, and the sheer joy of their music.

During spring and summer 1969, Twiggs and the band often crashed at my Atlanta apartment. I begged Twiggs to hire me, and he promised that the next open spot would be mine. He wanted to shed his road manager duties and continue as an equipment and stage manager. In November, the band released their self-titled debut album and in December made their first appearance at Bill Graham's Fillmore East in New York, opening for Blood, Sweat, & Tears. They played the Electric Factory in Philadelphia, then drove across the country to open for B. B. King and Buddy Guy at the Fillmore West and headline at the Whiskey A Go Go in Los Angeles. Then they drove back to New York for six shows with the Grateful Dead at the Fillmore East. I kept up with their movements and the progress of their album. I can recall an early ad in *Billboard* magazine that referred to their style as "swamp music"; the term "Southern rock" had yet to be coined. I kept my ears open, eagerly anticipating a call from Twiggs.

4

I Get the Call

O n April 30, 1970, I was shocked to read a wire service newspaper article concerning the stabbing death of a Buffalo, New York, club owner in a dispute over nonpayment of a band. Twiggs Lyndon was the alleged perpetrator, and he was being held on murder charges. A couple of days later, I received a call from Butch Trucks, one of The Allman Brothers Band's two drummers. The group was in Cleveland, working its way south, and Twiggs had told the band members that if anything ever happened to him, they were to call me with an invitation to take over the road manager's position. Would I meet the band at the upcoming show at Georgia Tech in Atlanta on May 9? You bet I would.

After the concert, I sat with the band in a Winnebago camper they had recently obtained for touring. I distinctly remember Duane telling me what a backbreaking job it would be and how crazy they all were. Still, if I wanted the job, it was mine. I told Duane

I would give my notice at the bank and be in Macon in two weeks.

By this time, I was doing fairly well as an auditor at the Trust Company of Georgia bank. I had apparently caught the eye of a few upper management types for several reasons. They were impressed with my audit reports. I predicted a branch robbery that occurred exactly as I described it. And I successfully handled security during the manufacturing of the bank's first credit cards. Some said I had a great head for commercial bank auditing. Others said I thought like a con man and bank robber. At any rate, I gave my two-week notice and never looked back. My employers, friends, and family could not fathom why I would give up a promising career in banking to work with a bunch of hippie musicians. I simply had a feeling that this would be one of the biggest bands in America. America just didn't know it yet.

Within days, I arrived at the Walden office and started getting to know the folks there. I had already met Phil Walden briefly on a couple of occasions through Twiggs. I remember being told that I wouldn't make much money at first, but that I'd "get more pussy than Frank Sinatra." I thought there was something to be said for that.

Later on, Roger Cowles, then Capricorn's publicity director, told me that he and others had taken bets on how long I would last. I had been a commercial banker and was about ten years older than most of the band and crew. They didn't think I'd be able to handle it. I proved them all wrong.

5

The Big House

The Big House really was a big house, with 19 rooms and 6,000 square feet of space. In 1900, Nathaniel E. Harris built it in the Grand Tudor style. Ironically, Harris served as the governor of Georgia from 1915 to 1917, just one term prior to that of my namesake and great uncle, Thomas William Hardwick. The house features high ceilings, intricate woodworking and wainscoting, and colorful stained glass windows on the staircase landings on all three of its floors. The wooded property outside features elaborate stonework, three fountains, and a large wraparound porch.

The first floor contains a formal foyer leading to a grand staircase, a parlor, a large living room with a fireplace, and a big screened-in sun porch that housed the band's equipment and was used as the rehearsal room. In addition to a kitchen and pantry is a formal dining room that at the time housed a stereo and was known as the music room. I took up residence in the living room, sleeping on a foldout couch.

The second floor offered separate living quarters for Duane, his wife Donna, and their daughter Galadrielle and for Berry, his wife Linda, and their young daughter Brittany, who was then better known by her affectionate nickname, "Bebop." Berry's younger sister Candace shared a bedroom with Gregg, her boyfriend at the time. Each band family was able to enjoy their private space. The second floor also houses a huge shower with seven spray heads, three on adjoining walls and one overhead, in addition to several other bathrooms.

The third floor had served as a small ballroom where Governor Harris held intimate concerts. We used it as a party room and even installed a full-sized professional pool table. During a recent visit, I marveled at how we had gotten that huge, heavy table all the way up the staircase of the three-story house.

Since none of the band members could afford personal telephones early on and had to visit neighbors or friends to make calls, I had a pay phone installed in the main floor foyer not too long after I moved in. It certainly improved communications both at home and on the road. Local phone calls cost only ten cents at the time, and a stack of dimes could usually be found on top of the phone. Since the band was often on the road, the ladies of the house handled household expenses.

The Big House was a comfortable place with a wonderful spirit of communal living. We were a family. The kids' toys were strewn around the house, and their high-pitched squeals resonated throughout the rooms. We sometimes ate home-cooked meals together. The top floor recreation room was a hangout for the band and crew and some of their friends.

I was warmly welcomed and made to feel at home. After a short while, I moved into a nearby apartment when my girlfriend and soon-to-be wife, Sandra, relocated to Macon from Atlanta.

Though my stay in the Big House was brief, I have great memories of my time there, especially the impromptu band rehearsals. I thoroughly enjoyed the abundant love and peacefulness of the home. What had been built as a prim and proper residence for Southern elite had been transformed into an informal, comfortable, warm, and loving home for several young families and a headquarters for an up-and-coming rock and roll band. The Big House would remain the center of the band's activities until shortly after Berry's death when, sadly, the remaining residents moved out. The spirit of the home instilled by the families and members of The Allman Brothers Band did not dissipate. You can still feel its presence when you walk through the front door.

Current band tour manager Kirk West and his wife Kirsten bought the Big House in the early 1990s and have made many needed repairs and improvements. Kirk has compiled a huge display of band memorabilia, which is displayed in the former band rehearsal room. The home is now the official repository of the band archives. Kirk and Kirsten hope to preserve it for all time through a tax-exempt foundation.

6

Crash Course

As my first show with the band approached, I took a self-taught crash course in road managing. I inherited Twiggs's briefcase along with boxes and envelopes full of receipts. Even though Twiggs had a reasonably good bookkeeping system, it would take me weeks to reconstruct and balance the books to get the band's accounting records on a sound footing. The band was basically broke and heavily in debt to their record label and management company for funds advanced for living expenses, vehicles, equipment, and personal and professional expenses. As the old sayings go, we were so broke we couldn't even pay attention, and the only thing we exchanged at Christmas was glances. It wouldn't be long before all that would change.

In those prehistoric days of rock, the road manager's job was massive. Generally, my duties were to pre-plan all the travel and lodging, make sure the band, crew, and equipment were at the place of engagement in time for setup and performance, get the band on and off the stage at the proper time, collect the money due from the promoter, and then get to the next town and do the same thing again, day after day. I had a great crew made up of Red Dog, Kim Payne, Mike Callahan, and, soon afterward, Joe Dan Petty. Later, Twiggs would rejoin the crew, and there would be many additions and deletions. I could have never succeeded without the help of those original guys.

When we were off the road, I had to post and balance the books, pay bills, make payrolls, and plan the next tour, plus basically be on twenty-four-hour call as a diplomat, logistician, amateur psychologist, disciplinarian, accountant, liaison with management and, if time allowed, have a personal life. All that and more for $90.00 a week before taxes, which is just what everyone else made. Earlier, when no one was getting salaries, Twiggs received a $50.00 weekly draw paid by the band as an advance from management. That practice continued when I was hired. When I realized I was making $140.00 weekly as opposed to everyone else making $90.00, I brought this to the band's attention. They didn't object, saying that I deserved it. Later, there would be differentials in salaries paid to the band and crew. Also, I asked Phil Walden to absorb the extra funds paid to Twiggs and me. He agreed over the objections of his bookkeeper.

Duane always insisted that the crew be paid first because he said that no matter how good the band was, they couldn't pull it off without the crew.

My first show was a high school graduation party on June 2, 1970, on Jekyll Island, Georgia. The Walden office sent Earl "Speedo" Simms to assist me in my debut. Speedo had been Otis Redding's road manager. Only by a quirk of fate was he not on Otis's final, fatal airplane flight. Speedo would also later join the Allman Brothers crew. He told me never to take my eyes off the road manager's briefcase because it contained all the current records of the band and, most importantly, all the cash. I had already learned one of Twiggs's tricks of handcuffing the briefcase to the bathroom sink or toilet pipes in hotel rooms. Over the years, many a young lady entering my hotel room would cast a nervous glance at those handcuffs attached to a briefcase and a pipe in the bathroom, wondering if they had any connection with events to come later in the evening. (More about the briefcase later.)

I also learned something else on my first show. I assumed all the band members would ride in the camper with Red Dog and me, while Mike Callahan and Kim Payne would travel together in the equipment truck. That wasn't to be, as most of the band was in Florida and would meet up at the gig. Over the years, I would have to deal with getting the band together for the first show of a tour from a myriad of locations. It was a nerve-wracking logistical nightmare, but we always managed it.

In those early days it was customary, if not mandatory, to be paid in cash. Generally, a promoter would post a cash deposit of fifty percent of the band's guaranteed fee with the booking agency. The road manager would pick up the balance of the guarantee plus any overage. Bands were and still are paid in several ways. There are flat guarantees of a specific amount, guarantees of a specific amount versus a percentage of the gross receipts (whichever is greater), guarantees of a specific amount plus a percentage of the gross receipts after expenses, or, rarely, no guarantee at all but a huge percentage of receipts after expenses. When dealing with club owners, many of whom were so crooked they could hide behind a corkscrew, I always collected cash in advance before I allowed the band to start the show. I also told them, "We have a deal with the bank. They don't play rock and roll and we don't take checks."

Two early shows were exceptions to the "cash only" rule. The Cosmic Carnival in Atlanta at the Braves baseball stadium on June 13, 1970, boasted a tremendous lineup including Traffic, Frank Zappa, Ike and Tina Turner, Mountain, Ten Years After, and others. For some reason, the show didn't sell well and many of the acts chose not to perform. The promoter, Forrest Hamilton, explained his plight to me and to Bunky Odom, a representative of the Walden office. He would not be able to pay us the balance of our fee, but he begged us to play to avoid a riot of those in attendance. There was no way the band was going to walk out on an Atlanta crowd, so we agreed. The band also announced that they would play for free the next day in Piedmont Park to make up for the acts that didn't perform.

In addition, the promoter insisted that Duane not invite the crowd out of the stands and onto the field, just as Duane good-naturedly and unknowingly told the crowd, "By the way, why don't y'all come down on the field where you can see and hear better." We left poor Forrest sitting in the Braves dugout with his head in his hands as the crowd poured over the railings and onto the playing field. The band did play for free in the park the next day as promised, solidifying themselves as the "peoples' band" and "Atlanta's band." Four years later on June 1, 1974, we played that same Atlanta stadium before a record crowd of 61,232 and walked out with $233,097.20. Barely.

After the free Piedmont Park show, we made a quick run to Florida for four shows, then back to the Atlanta suburb of Marietta for one more show before the next big one, the second Atlanta Pop Festival. It was held outdoors at a speedway in Byron, Georgia, near Macon. We were the unofficial host band for the three-day event, which featured a lineup including Jimi Hendrix, Johnny Winter, B. B. King, and many others. The Allman Brothers Band would open the show on Friday in 100-plus-degree heat and play again in the relative cool of early Monday morning. Duane had been in Miami finishing up work on the band's second album at Criteria Studios, but he assured me he would arrive in plenty of time. As our performance time drew closer, Duane still had not shown up; I began to worry. Finally, he appeared at the backstage gate, riding on the back seat of a commandeered motorcycle. His car had gotten caught in a huge traffic jam on Interstate 75. Traffic had backed up for miles in both directions, but Duane had charmed his way onto the back of a bike, which raced down the shoulder of the highway to the gig. We would retrieve Duane's abandoned car later.

That traffic jam was a preview of the hordes that would descend on tiny Byron. Soon, the gates were crashed and liberated. The promoters were unable to sell any more tickets, and they officially declared it a free festival. Alex Cooley and his partners eventually took a huge financial hit, and there was a shortage of cash. Of course, there was no way the band would refuse to play for several hundred thousand fans, and we went on as scheduled.

I was assured that there were limited funds in the promoter's account, but I knew the chances were high that the check would bounce if I deposited it through normal banking channels. When I saw that the account was with my old employer, the Trust Company of Georgia, I accepted it. On Monday morning, after being awake for practically three days straight, I jumped into my car and raced to Atlanta to get there when the bank opened. The check was good, and I got cash for the band. I'm sure other check holders were not so fortunate. Alex Cooley went on to be one of the most respected promoters in the South, and I'm sure he made amends to everyone involved.

One other festival of note in my first months with the band was the Love Valley Festival. Love Valley, North Carolina, was an unusual venue. It was like a movie set of a Western town, except the buildings were real instead of false facades. Its one dirt street led to the outdoor rodeo arena, a natural amphitheater that would be our concert site. This was a multi-day event with mostly regional bands; The Allman Brothers Band was one of the headliners. This was also the only time the original band was captured on film to any great degree. I say on film because the soundtrack to this performance was somehow lost. There were plans to release a film of the festival, but they fell through. I have heard recently that the producer of the film is deceased and the 35-millimeter negative of the footage is now lost as well. The ABB archives contain a bootleg video copy of some of the footage with a non-synched amateur audiotape of "Mountain Jam."

The band made friends with the Barker family, who owned the property and promoted the show. We "lay dead" there, as the band would say, on two different occasions that summer—once when the Winnebago camper broke down and again when a festival up north was canceled as we were en route. Dickey Betts became so enamored with the place that he briefly stayed at a remote cabin there, far out in the woods without a phone. I used to have to call the main house with Dickey's flight information when we flew. The Barkers' young son would take the information out to Dickey by horseback. I'm guessing I was the only road manager using the "Pony Express" to deliver messages in 1970.

7

Tour, Tour, Tour, and a Fateful Meeting

After the Love Valley Festival, the band settled into a backbreaking schedule of nonstop touring. We were rarely home in Macon for more than a few days at a time. The second album wouldn't be completed until August and released in late September, so there was little, if any, Allman Brothers music on the radio at the time. Constant touring fueled the band's growing popularity. We went up and down the east coast repeatedly like a mail carrier on his daily route and played more than a hundred concerts between June and December. When we weren't playing for pay, the band would jam for free. If there weren't any gigs, Duane would fly to New York or Miami for outside sessions or to finish up work on the band's second album, *Idlewild South* (named for a lakeside cabin outside Macon that was briefly a band home).

In August, we played Greensboro, Raleigh, Greensboro again, Martinsville, Fayetteville, Philadelphia, Boston, Norfolk, Savannah, Jacksonville Beach, Miami Beach, Melbourne, and three shows in Pensacola. Prior to the Miami Beach show, Duane called producer Tom Dowd, who had just started recording with Eric Clapton in Miami, and invited him to the show. It was an outdoor event, and a security barricade stood between the crowd and the stage with a small space in between. About halfway into the show, we saw Tom Dowd, Eric, and some or all of the Dominos—which consisted of Bobby Whitlock, Carl Radle, and Jim Gordon—crawling into the space in front of the stage. Duane was so floored that he momentarily stopped playing. Of course, the concertgoers could see none of this and had no idea what was going on.

After the concert, we all went over to Criteria Studios. Eric had heard of Duane from Wilson Pickett's "Hey Jude" sessions, and Duane was familiar with Eric primarily from Eric's work with Cream. There was definitely mutual respect and admiration between the two of them. I can distinctly remember sitting on the studio floor as Tom Dowd played back some tracks from the band's album in progress, *Idlewild South*. Eric especially loved Duane's slide work on "Don't Keep Me Wonderin'." At some point, there was a jam with Duane, Dickey, and Eric on guitars, Gregg and Bobby Whitlock on keyboards, Berry on bass, and Butch on drums. It's included on the CD box set *The Layla Sessions*, 20th Anniversary Edition.

I think it's safe to say that Duane was the catalyst for the Layla album that followed. He was invited to play and promised to return to Miami as soon as he finished the current run of dates. We had about four days off between Pensacola and Milwaukee, and Duane headed straight back to Miami as promised. Then he begged off of the two shows in Milwaukee and two more in Chicago because things were going so well in the studio. This caused a minor bit of friction among the band members, and I had a hard time explaining to the club owners why The Allman Brothers Band had only one Allman brother in it. When we all got back to Macon, a meeting was held with the band, Phil Walden, and Duane, who agreed not to let any future outside projects interfere with the band's career. As I recall, he said, "We've got our own fish to fry," and the band came first.

When the Layla sessions were completed, Duane showed up at the Walden office in a state of euphoria. He said he had just been having fun, but in addition to his union scale session fees, he had gotten some cash; I think it was around $1,500.00. Phil Walden noted that fun was fun, but that Duane should be fairly compensated, and he negotiated a royalty participation for Duane from Clapton's management. I believe Duane's first check was for several thousand dollars, and, as I recall, he bought a brand new Volvo with some of the proceeds.

The nonstop touring continued into fall 1970. Most of the shows were at clubs, music halls, and colleges. Occasionally, there were opening or "special guest star" slots on major shows. We opened for Grand Funk Railroad at an outdoor stadium show in Washington, D.C., and received $4,000.00, a princely sum at that point. We also played what would turn out to be the last free concert at Piedmont Park in Atlanta. The park could no longer handle the crowds, and we were unable to get the newly required permits without a hassle.

In late September, we returned to the Fillmore East in New York for a PBS/NET television special taping. These tapes were long thought lost or erased, but copies have surfaced and been restored. They provide a rare look at what the original band was like in a live concert setting. We would return to the Fillmore in December, second billed to Canned Heat for four shows.

On October 30, we received the scare of our young rock and roll lives when Duane accidentally overdosed on opium after a show in Nashville. He was admitted to Vanderbilt University Hospital, and it was touch and go for several hours before his condition stabilized. We were up all night, but once we were sure Duane was going to be all right, we drove on to Atlanta for a concert at Emory University without Duane, who was held in the hospital for observation. A sheepish and contrite Duane Allman joined us the next day for a concert in Charlotte, promising that would never, ever happen again. Although Duane was far from finished experimenting with drugs, I don't recall another incident that harrowing while we were on the road.

Duane also found time to appear with Delaney and Bonnie at Carnegie Hall in New York, with Derek and the Dominos in Tampa and Syracuse, and as a player during sessions with Ronnie Hawkins back at Criteria Studios in Miami with producer Tom Dowd. The year came to a close with a show at the Warehouse music hall in New Orleans, which would become one of our favorite venues. The second album was receiving great reviews and respectable, though not spectacular, airplay and sales. My first six months with The Allman Brothers Band had been exhilarating and exhausting, and I had a sense that the band was on the verge of breaking big. Little did I know what triumphs and heartbreak lay ahead in the new year.

8

Bunking with Duane

My first policy clash with the band came over hotel rooms. They wanted to rent as many as possible, and I wanted to rent as few as possible. My touring philosophy was one of "economy with dignity." I tried to make touring as comfortable as possible at the lowest cost to the band. I figured that every dollar I saved on touring was a dollar that could go to some other purpose to benefit the band. Twiggs had even told me that one of the reasons for getting the Winnebago camper was to save on hotel rooms since it had several comfortable bunks. So we compromised by usually renting one or two rooms.

Years later, Red Dog told me that early on, when there were complaints about me being too strict, Duane lined everyone up military fashion and told them to stick with me because he felt I would prove to be an asset to the band. I regret not finding that out until Duane was gone. I never got a chance to thank him for his vote of confidence.

I also learned another good early lesson from Red Dog. Once, when I berated him harshly in front of the band for arriving late for a trip departure, he took me aside and said it was fair to jump on him for being late but not to show him up in front of the band. I've always tried to remember that when it was necessary to discipline someone for screwing up.

A genuine brotherhood and communal spirit existed among the band, crew, and their families at this time. It was primarily based around the music, but it went a lot deeper. We really did love one another and were dead serious about bringing the band's spirit and music to the masses. I dedicated myself to this premise 100 percent, 24/7, 365 days a year, often to the detriment of my personal life and my relationships with family and friends.

As finances improved through fall 1970 and into 1971, we were able to get to the point where we bunked two to a room. Originally, I bunked with Jaimoe most of the time. A kinder and sweeter man never walked this earth. I will always remember him insisting that I send a portion of his earnings home to his mother in Mississippi every week. Duane usually roomed with Berry, but more and more as time went by, he began to double up with me on many trips. I guessed this might have been because there was less all-night partying in my room. The phone usually rang incessantly, however, and people knocked on my door twenty-four hours a day, so it wasn't exactly an oasis of tranquility.

Duane did not have much of a formal education, but he was self-educated and street smart and he "got it." He and I used to joke that we both were "roads scholars" as opposed to "Rhodes Scholars." He was a vociferous reader, especially of fantasy novels, and he enjoyed the works of J. R. R. Tolkien such as *The Hobbit*, *The Fellowship of the Ring*, and others. His daughter Galadrielle is named after a Tolkien character, although he changed the spelling from Galadriel because, according to Donna Allman, "Duane thought it sounded more French." Another of his favorites was the Conan the Barbarian series by Robert E. Howard, a pulp fiction author of the 1920s and 1930s. Critics and fans have noted that Conan was not strictly a hero or do-gooder, but rather someone who followed his own code of honor and tried to stay alive in a world full of peril. I think Duane ascribed to that philosophy, and I have tried to as well. Duane also enjoyed reading some of the more literate comic books of the day, including Stan Lee's Marvel Comics characters Spider-Man, The Fantastic Four, Silver Surfer, Mighty Thor, and The Incredible Hulk. These comics offered real substance and social commentary, and Duane recognized it. He also enjoyed the biting satire of the underground comics of Robert Crump, featuring the cult icons Mr. Natural and Fritz the Cat. Duane once told me that if he really enjoyed reading something, he would read it over and over again. I have found myself doing the same thing through the years.

When he wasn't reading, Duane was often concentrating on his music. I can see him now sitting on the side of a motel bed playing his acoustic guitar either alone or with Dickey, Berry, or visiting musicians who joined him. Duane had many musical influences. Around this time, he was really into Miles Davis and John Coltrane. Most people probably don't know that one of his favorite songs, as well as mine, was Clarence Carter's version of Jim Webb's "Do What You Gotta Do." Gregg and Cher later recorded their version as a duo on the album *Allman and Woman, Two the Hard Way.*

When fans would rave that he was a guitar god, Duane would laugh and tell them there were unknown players everywhere working in tiny dives who could play circles around him. It was a generous gesture on his part, but I didn't believe him for a minute.

Duane was also very discrete and circumspect in his liaisons with the ladies. There was no blatant womanizing by him. That just wasn't his style.

I have only one memory of going to the movies with Duane. In summer 1971 on the boardwalk of Atlantic City, we saw *Summer of '42.* Duane was especially moved by this bittersweet, nostalgic tale of a teenager coming of sexual age during summer vacation and his adolescent crush on an older war bride. I think we both fell in love with the natural beauty of Jennifer O'Neil.

Of course, we saw a lot of movies together on television in the hotels. At the Hyatt on Sunset Boulevard in Los Angeles, we discovered the absolutely enchanting 1940 Technicolor version of *The Thief of Baghdad*. It remains one of the all-time great screen fantasies, and I never tire of watching it. Duane loved the anarchy of Marx Brothers films, and he always commented on the musicianship of Harpo. He also enjoyed the old Sherlock Holmes movies starring Basil Rathbone and Nigel Bruce. I don't think Duane cared much for regular television fare in those days of three networks and no remote controls. At least New York, Los Angeles, and San Francisco offered some channels with all-night programming, and Cincinnati had a great Saturday all-night horror film host who seemed to get drunker as the evening progressed.

Duane did love the satire of *All in the Family*, especially Carroll O'Connor's portrayal of Archie Bunker. The series originally aired on Wednesday nights at 9:30, but it soon moved to Saturday evenings at 8:00, when we'd watch it right before heading to the night's gig. I can still see Duane's bemused expression reacting to Archie's boldfaced bigotry.

I never tired of Duane's wit, wisdom, sense of humor, humility, and love of life. He had that rare talent of seeming to know what life was all about. He had a natural bullshit detector and did not suffer fools gladly as many an interviewer and photographer can attest. Of course, Duane was not infallible, but usually when he made a mistake, he learned from it and rarely repeated it. He also took sincere criticism well, listened carefully to the advice of older hands in the music business, and spent a lot of time at Phil Walden's home. They developed a special professional relationship and friendship.

On the subject of drugs, it is no secret that Duane experimented wildly during the time I knew him. I believe it was a combination of his curiosity, the culture of the times, and the natural penchant for musicians to indulge. During our times together, I was not using drugs (that would come later), and Duane never openly flaunted his drug use in front of me. He specifically warned me not to try heroin, saying I would probably enjoy it initially, and to this day I've followed his advice. I believe that at the time of his death, Duane had overcome his dependence on heroin, though he still continued to use cocaine. At that time, recreational cocaine use was not thought to be particularly destructive. I do believe that had he lived, Duane would have outgrown his drug use. He was just too smart and too strong to let anything control him for long.

Finally, one of my fondest memories of Duane was his natural affection. I guess one of my personal hang-ups was that I tended to stiffen up when hugged by members of either sex. Outright expressions of affection did not come easily for me. Duane, though, was a real hugger, and he would laugh at my half-hearted responses to his friendly physical displays of affection, telling me to loosen up. Duane, old buddy, I'm still trying to loosen up. And I'm getting better at it.

9

More of the Same

After taking the first week of 1971 off, we immediately resumed our nonstop touring with a run of colleges in the South. Then, on January 16, we made a triumphant return to Atlanta for two sold-out shows at the 5,000-seat municipal auditorium. Our guarantee was $5,000.00, but we packed the place to the rafters and took home an additional $6,213.00 in overage money, the band's biggest payday to date. The next day, we were in Pittsburgh for a great concert with Macon's own Little Richard and Taj Mahal. The colorful poster for that show is a rare collector's item valued by some at about $3,500.00, exactly what the band received for their performance. We then proceeded to Portchester, New York, just north of New York City, for a two-day run at the Capitol Theater. Poor-quality amateur tapes exist of those shows, but the performances were memorable. An old Southern saying about sex goes, "The worst I ever had was wonderful."

The same could be said for the band's performances. On their worst nights, the energy and musicianship were still incredibly good, but on the nights when they were really on fire, the experience was nothing short of magic.

Our touring schedule began to require more and more flying, and after a couple of more shows, we flew to the west coast for concerts at the Fillmore West in San Francisco and the Whiskey A Go Go in Los Angeles. At the Fillmore, we were the middle act on a show headlined by Hot Tuna and opened by the Trinidad Tripoli Steel Band, another great combination put together by Bill Graham. The poster for that show is also a valuable collector's item. I once had a huge stack of the originals, but they are nowhere to be found now. As W. C. Fields would say, "Drat!"

During one early trip to San Francisco, we all got the ABB mushroom logo tattoos applied to our calves by famed tattoo artist Lyle Tuttle. At the time it was sort of a goof, but over the years it has become a badge of honor and tradition for most new members of the band and crew. Later on, we had a little dust-up with a still relatively unknown rock photographer, Annie Liebowitz. She had been assigned by *Rolling Stone* magazine to accompany us on a drive down the coast in rental cars as part of a photo shoot. At a stop along the road, she asked the band members to roll up their pants legs for a photo of the mushroom tattoos. Duane exploded and would have nothing of it. It was just too bogus for his taste. To her credit, however, she did take classic shots of the band, the most notable being one of Duane and Gregg sleeping in the back of a rental car.

Returning to the Whiskey A Go Go in Los Angeles was sort of a homecoming for Duane and Gregg. They had performed there many times as members of Hour Glass, and they had lots of old friends in the city as well. This was my first trip to the west coast, and I grew to love our periodic visits there. I believe we had our first ever ride in a limousine, courtesy of Atlantic Records, Capricorn's distributor. In the years to follow, we would have fleets of limos on twenty-four-hour call. The owner of Head Limo, a trendy limo service in New York, told me he had to give his drivers a week off to recover from mental and physical exhaustion after the Allman Brothers left town.

We finished in Los Angeles on February 3, and the next night we had a concert at Ohio Wesleyan University in Delaware, Ohio. This was one of our famous "dartboard" tour jumps when I accused the agency of throwing darts at a map of the U.S. and then booking us wherever the darts struck. Although Phil Walden's Paragon Agency booked us in the southeastern states, Associated Booking Corporation now booked us nationally. With principal offices in New York, Chicago, and Beverly Hills, ABC, as it was called, was primarily an R&B agency, and B. B. King was their longtime client. Old-timer Joe Glaser, who directed the career of

Louis "Satchmo" Armstrong, founded ABC. Jon Podell, who was a young agent there at the time, is still involved in booking the band. Later, Paragon would take over all the bookings again, although Phil Walden negotiated the terms for most of the bigger dates himself.

Flying back-to-back gigs created a logistical nightmare. The band would not play on rental equipment, so if there was no time to drive their equipment to the next gig, it would have to fly as well. This required us to truck our equipment to the airfreight terminal at the departure city and have another rental truck at the destination city to pick it up. Often, the band-owned equipment truck would have to dead head empty to some catch-up point down the road several gigs ahead. Gregg's Hammond B-3 organ case would not fit through the cargo doors on some DC-9's, which were widely used at the time, and that meant the equipment might be placed on a separate flight.

The band also refused to check their guitars as baggage, which required us to buy one additional seat referred to as "cabin baggage," where Duane's, Berry's, and Dickey's instruments were dutifully strapped into a seat using a seat belt extension designed for large passengers. Two of my all-time favorite 1971 jumps by air were from Burlington, Vermont, in the afternoon to Rindge, New Hampshire, for an evening performance. It wasn't far, but we flew in February during a blinding snowstorm. Somehow, Mike Callahan and Kim Payne got the equipment truck to the venue on icy two-lane back roads. I flew the rest of the crew and the band on a tiny prop commuter plane during a complete whiteout blizzard with our landing gear frozen in the up position. All I could think of was another February day when Buddy Holly, Richie Valens, and the Big Bopper made a similar flight. The other thriller was in September 1971, when we overnighted from Montreal, Canada, to Miami, Florida. Clearing customs going in and out of Canada and back into the U.S. was memorable. On another occasion customs officers were bemused and puzzled to discover Twiggs's double-ended dildo in his luggage. I guess we were stupid and crazy to take some of these jumps, but I loved the challenge, and the band and crew never failed to do their part. Our motto was "The difficult we do immediately; the impossible takes longer."

Another interesting facet of flying commercial was the reaction of our fellow travelers. We were quite a bizarre-looking bunch in those days, as the average business traveler hadn't had much exposure to rock musicians. Once, a prominent Maconite upgraded his entire family from coach to first class in order to escape contact with the hippie-looking denizens he encountered at the departure gate. Imagine his chagrin when we were the only other passengers in first class!

By the end of February 1971, we had performed approximately forty more shows, and even though the second album had only been out for a few months, we were busy formulating plans to capture the power of the band in a live recording. There was no better way to communicate to the masses just how powerful the band had become.

10

Live at the Fillmore East

Live albums had typically been "throwaways." At that time, two notable exceptions were a Ray Charles album recorded at the Newport Jazz Festival and James Brown recorded at the Apollo Theater in New York. Live album content was often a re-recorded version of previously released studio material. The quality of the recordings and the performances was usually inferior to the studio versions. It was felt, however, that a live recording would capture the essence of The Allman Brothers Band and translate into increased album sales.

Phil Walden and the band not only wanted a live album, but Phil insisted on a two-disc album, specially priced at $6.98, the normal cost for a single album at that time. Atlantic Records was against this concept for all the reasons outlined above, plus they wanted the extra cost pricing that a double-disc album normally got. Additionally, Frank Fenter of Capricorn had to cut deals with music publishers of outside material to keep the mechanical rights fees within bounds. Phil was adamant, and he eventually prevailed. Tom Dowd was to produce and record the band's performances at the Fillmore East in New York on March 12 and 13, 1971.

The first night's recording was a near disaster, almost scuttling the entire project. The band had gotten the idea to include two horn player friends of Jaimoe as well as a harp player, Thom Doucette. Doucette had previously sat in with the band on occasion and was not a problem. I was aghast, however, at the idea of the horn players because it was so contrary to the normal sound of the band that we hoped to capture, but the group did not seek my creative opinions and Capricorn wasn't even aware of the plan. Well, it didn't work, and Tom Dowd went ballistic. He didn't know anything about the horn players, was not set up to track them, and didn't like the sound at all. After the show, he and the band reviewed the night's results, and they mutually agreed that the horn players would not return for Saturday night's show. Things went much better the next night, and enough quality material was recorded to include in the follow-up album as well.

I am often asked about the cover photo for the album. The original concept for the cover was a photo of the Fillmore marquee with the band's name on it. Those pictures were taken and prints of them exist. The format was changed to the final concept of band and crew on the front and back covers. Photographer Jim Marshall took the photos in an alleyway near Capricorn

Studios in Macon. The shot of the band used on the cover was taken immediately after Duane seated himself upon returning from a mission to secure some contraband and, yes, the goods are firmly grasped in his left hand. The impish smile on his face says it all as the rest of the band roars in laughter. The photographer fumed but managed to capture perfectly the personalities of the band members. The back cover was a shot of the road crew, including myself, with an insert of Twiggs (who was still in confinement).

The mixed and mastered album was delivered in June and officially released on July 6, 1971. The rest, as they say, is history. Capricorn's marketing strategy proved brilliant, and a breathtaking musical performance was captured in the grooves. The album was released to rave reviews and was a resounding, runaway sales success. Thirty-plus years later, it stands the test of time and is on every serious list of the greatest rock recordings ever made.

11

Busted

We left New York in triumph, not knowing we would all be in jail before the month ended. After one additional show at a community college in Connecticut, our next gig was in New Orleans for two nights at The Warehouse, a huge old cotton warehouse with great atmosphere. Then our plans called for traveling in rental cars to Lafayette, Louisiana, and on to shows in Alabama before flying up to Minneapolis and then back to the northeast.

I had instructed the drivers to take an indirect route to our destination, mostly via Interstate 65, because I didn't relish the idea of our little caravan traveling the back roads of Alabama all night. I remember nodding off in one of the rental cars somewhere around Biloxi, listening to the ethereal strains of "In Memory of Elizabeth Reed" from a New Orleans radio station. It was always a treat to hear the band's recordings on the radio. I had subsequently fallen into a deep sleep when the lead vehicle made a wrong turn near Mobile and headed directly up the road I had wanted to avoid.

My first realization that something was terribly wrong came when Joe Dan Petty awakened me. We were in the parking lot of a restaurant near Grove Hill and Jackson, Alabama, and a massive bust was going down. As best I can recall and reconstruct, here's what happened.

Our two rental cars and equipment truck had stopped at a restaurant shortly after daybreak. David "Tuffy" Phillips was driving the equipment truck instead of the usual roadies; Mike Callahan was ill, and Kim Payne was recovering from gunshot wounds administered by a Macon cop during a "routine" traffic stop. Some of us slept in the vehicles while others went inside to eat. Red Dog, Berry Oakley, and Dickey Betts remained in one car until Dickey got out and Berry noticed him behaving somewhat erratically. He got Dickey back into the car and pulled the vehicle to the side of the restaurant where they couldn't be observed from within. Then Dickey got back out of the car and started wandering into the woods. Berry again got out to try to settle him down. At some point, the police were alerted to our presence, and an officer approached Berry and Dickey. He started to question Dickey, then approached the car where Red Dog was sleeping and began a search, which revealed a vial of marijuana and some antibiotic pills. By the time I woke up, one officer was telling me he was arresting Dickey and Red Dog.

He put Dickey and myself in the back of his patrol car and Berry and Red Dog in another and then went to talk to the rest of the band and crew. At some point, Gregg went to one of our cars, removed some contraband, and went back into the restaurant and flushed it down the toilet. He still had a glassine envelope in his wallet, and a filled marijuana pipe was in the car.

At this point, Red Dog discovered a stash of hallucinogens in his pocket and handed them to Berry, who called Joe Dan to the police car and handed it over with instructions to flush it and then clean out whatever else remained in the cars. Joe Dan went back into the restaurant and accomplished the flushing, but by the time he returned, the police had secured the rental cars.

So Dickey and I sat in one police car, Berry and Red Dog sat in the other, and we were about to be driven to the Jackson police headquarters. We learned that the officer driving the second car was named Jethro, I kid you not. A civilian assisting the two officers drove the equipment truck. Jethro instructed Duane, Gregg, Butch, Jaimoe, Joe Dan, and Tuffy to join the procession into town in the rental cars. Gregg then threw his glassine envelope and the filled pipe out of the car window. The pipe was never found, but after we arrived in town, an elderly citizen walked into the police station with a glassine envelope that he saw being thrown out one of the car windows. While the individual could not identify the culprit, the envelope was later alleged to contain heroin. Then all of us were placed in jail cells and search warrants were issued for the vehicles. Dickey's still erratic behavior so alarmed the authorities that they wanted him out of public view. Accompanied by Joe Dan Petty, he was transferred unsupervised to the sheriff's residence. Later, when the sheriff called his wife at home on a personal matter, he was annoyed when Dickey answered the phone.

Eventually, charges were filed against various individuals for possession of marijuana, heroin, and phencyclidine (a type of animal tranquilizer that, in later discussions among ourselves, nobody admitted to possessing).

My first task was to get us out of jail and out of town as soon as possible. No Alabama bail bondsman would handle us directly, but the Walden office was able to arrange bail through the Genone brothers' bail bondsmen back in Macon.

The next day, we were released and headed for that night's show at the University of Alabama in Tuscaloosa. Amazingly, we discovered that the luggage and guitar cases were still filled with controlled substances, which I encouraged the band members to dispose of immediately. They did so by consuming most of it then and there.

Condon, Kloche, Ange, Gervase, and Sedita was a venerable criminal law firm in Buffalo, New York. Phil Walden had originally retained them years earlier when entertainer Arthur Conley was detained in Buffalo on a firearms possession charge. They later represented Twiggs when he went on trial in New York for first-degree murder of the club manager, facing life imprisonment.

John Condon, a charming gentleman, was the lead attorney and a brilliant lawyer. He was a composite of every great trial attorney ever seen in real life, on TV, or in the movies. In Twiggs's case, his theory was that Twiggs was not guilty by reason of temporary insanity deep-seated since childhood, and that the stress of touring, drug use, and working with the band had pushed him over the edge. Condon had also maneuvered a non-jury trial over a caught-off-guard prosecutor, and his witnesses included an obviously drug-intoxicated Berry Oakley. The verdict was not guilty by reason of temporary insanity, an extremely rare occurrence. Twiggs was admitted to a mental facility in New York where he amazed the staff. One of his accomplishments was inducing a fellow patient to speak for the first time in many years. Twiggs was soon discharged, and after a little rest at home he came back to work as head of the stage crew and production manager.

John Condon and a bright young attorney, Joe Sedita, represented us in Alabama. After much discussion and negotiation, an increased cash bond was posted. The felony drug charges were replaced with non-extraditable misdemeanor charges. All charges against Joe Dan Petty and me were dropped. The remaining defendants did not appear at trial, the cash bond was forfeited, and that was the end of the matter. It would not be our last contact with attorney John Condon.

12

Lady Luck and the Slide Bottle

Duane played his distinctive slide style using a glass bottle in which the over-the-counter cold remedy Coricidin was sold. One of my responsibilities was to assure that Duane always had one on hand. When he took his last slide solo at the end of the show, he would place the bottle on Gregg's organ. Invariably, a fan would grab it as the roadies broke down the equipment. If I weren't tied up elsewhere, I would grab it myself and put it in the moneybag in my briefcase. When we ran out of them, I would buy a bottle of Coricidin at a drug store, dump the pills, and soak the label off in a hotel lavatory.

Once in New York, prior to a Fillmore show, I was frantically taking care of pre-gig business, including dashing across the street from the One Fifth Avenue Hotel to buy a slide bottle from the drug store for the night's show. Upon returning to the hotel, I was just about to head up the elevator when I realized to my absolute horror that I had left my briefcase, which contained thousands of dollars in cash, on the floor of the drug store at the checkout counter. My God, I was ruined! I knew it would take the rest of my life to repay the band all their money, not to mention the fact that we would have to take care of our current finances. My heart was in my throat as I ran back across the street to the drug store, knowing the chances of recovering the briefcase intact, in New York, were virtually nil. But there it was, untouched and unmolested right where I had left it! Old lady luck had smiled on the band and me that day. She would not always do so.

Immediately upon returning to Macon, I contacted the Schering-Plough Corporation, manufacturers of Coricidin, and explained how we used their bottles. They were gracious enough to send me, at no cost, a whole case of empty, unlabeled bottles. It would turn out to be a lifetime supply.

13

Happy Birthday

In retrospect, it's amazing that none of us seemed to have any fears about the serious drug charges hanging over our heads. We resumed our frenzied touring, and the band's drug use did not subside. April 1971 was our biggest month to date as the band grossed $73,962.00 for seventeen dates, an average of $4,350.00 per show. That is puny by today's standards, but it was tremendous at the time.

On April 17 at the Ramada Inn in Charlotte, Duane asked me for a salary advance of more than a hundred dollars. I explained to him that he had already drawn his entire salary for the week and that he shouldn't go over into the next week. He told me not to worry about it, just give him the cash. When I did, he handed it back to me and said, "Happy birthday, and make sure you charge me personally and not the band." That was my only birthday spent working with Duane, and I never forgot his thoughtful gesture. On another occasion, I complimented him on a beautiful handmade jacket that an admirer made for him and he immediately took it off his back, insisting that I take it. On my one-year anniversary of working for the band, he held a mock "twenty years of service in one year" ceremony and gave me a gold Swiss pocket watch with a beautiful carving depicting a cattle drive. Duane's kindness and generosity certainly weren't limited to me; time and time again I saw similar acts directed toward others he cared about.

The touring continued into May, although Duane found time on some off days in New York to do a session with Herbie Mann and sit in with the Grateful Dead at the Fillmore. Also in May, we were excited to receive the band's first artist royalty check from Atlantic Records for $9,422.77. Again, that is miniscule by today's standards, but it was huge at the time. Next, we received the shocking news that Bill Graham was closing the Fillmore East, and we would headline the final shows.

14

The Closing of the Fillmore East

It was unfathomable to us at the time that Bill Graham would close both the Fillmore East and West, the meccas for rock bands and a special home for The Allman Brothers Band.

Graham was a lover of the arts and a true showman, but first and foremost he was a businessman. As the rock music business grew out of its infancy, band managers and booking agents began seeking higher guarantees and percentages for their acts. Bill Graham probably paid less than any other major promoter at the time, partially dictated by the size of his venues. The Fillmore East had a capacity of just 2,654. With ticket prices of $3.50, $4.50, and $5.50, the gross for one show topped out at about $12,575.00. A normal two-day, four-show engagement grossed around $50,000.00, of which the headliner earned only about $12,000.00. This was not a huge four-show payday by any means, especially in New York City. The truth of the matter was that Bill Graham faced a profit squeeze, and more and more managers moved their acts to different promoters at higher-paying venues. Graham, I think, felt a certain amount of bitterness over what he considered a lack of loyalty, but the handwriting was on the wall. At the time, I believe he said he was retiring from active promotion to concentrate on artist management, but he came back to produce many more shows and tours, continuing right up until the time of his death as he left a show in a helicopter at one of his outdoor venues.

We were thrilled and honored to be part of the closing festivities at the Fillmore East and headlined shows on Friday and Saturday, June 25 and 26, 1971, supported by the J. Geils Band and Albert King. The final show on Sunday night, June 27, was, as I recall, an invitation-only performance with no tickets sold. In addition to the three bands from Friday and Saturday's bill, Mountain, Edgar Winter, Country Joe and the Fish, and the Beach Boys were added. The legendary but overly self-important Beach Boys demanded that they close the show and threatened to pack up and leave if they didn't. Graham called their bluff and told them to go ahead and leave because the Allmans were closing. They decided to play as scheduled, and the Allmans did close with an earthshaking set that lasted for hours. This was not the first weekend I had walked out of the Fillmore into the morning light, but, alas, it was the last.

15

Headed for a Fall

July was a light touring month, and we took some well-deserved time off. We had been invited to perform at the prestigious Newport Jazz Festival, one of the few rock bands ever to receive such an invitation. All of the band members were thrilled and honored. We had just checked into our hotel the night before the band's scheduled performance when we saw on local TV that unruly fans had created a disturbance at one of the events. Local officials deemed it a riot, and the remaining performances were cancelled. This was a huge disappointment to us, and especially to Duane. He had looked forward to playing at that festival.

Duane stayed busy on our rare time off. He did more sessions with Herbie Mann and did a show with Delaney and Bonnie and Friends along with Gregg and King Curtis; it was broadcast on WPLJ-FM radio in New York. The Allman Brothers Band would later do a similar broadcast. Duane would also do an interview for

Cream magazine and more sessions back in Macon with Capricorn artists Cowboy. Shortly thereafter, the senseless murder of King Curtis touched him deeply, and he played at Curtis's funeral along with artists like Aretha Franklin and Stevie Wonder. At some point around this time, Duane mentioned to Phil Walden that he was living on the edge and that Phil would be wise not to bet all his chips on Duane being around forever. At about the same time, Duane was telling us that the band finally had it made.

We were beginning to feel like we indeed had it made. The band was getting recognition, and we were playing more of the major market cities. Performance guarantees were now routinely in the $7,500.00 to $10,000.00 range, and as fall approached, we scheduled big tours that covered the Midwest, Southwest, and West Coast. On our west coast tour, a writer for *Rolling Stone* magazine joined us. This was to be their first major story on the band, but the rapport with the writer was terrible and the article proved to be a major disappointment.

A couple of years later we had a positive experience with *Rolling Stone* magazine when their teenage phenom writer Cameron Crowe wrote a favorable cover story on the band. He went on to be a successful film-maker and directed the definitive rock and roll movie, *Almost Famous*, based in part on his experience with The Allman Brothers Band.

On October 17, we played our last date of the tour at Painters Mill Music Fair outside Baltimore. It was a fairly routine gig, although the band was frantically awaiting the arrival of their source for a big score of heroin. We received a $10,000.00 fee. It was the last public performance Duane Allman made with The Allman Brothers Band.

16

The Passing of Duane

We were due to resume work in early November, but it was obvious that something had to be done about the band's increasingly destructive use of heroin. Everybody in the band and crew except for me had gotten themselves into trouble with drugs and alcohol to one degree or another. Duane, Berry, Gregg, Red Dog, Kim, and others went to Linwood-Bryant Hospital in Buffalo, New York, under the auspices of Phil Walden through John Condon's law offices. Others, including Joe Dan and Dickey, cold-turkeyed on their own. The intermediate and long-term value of this cleanup interlude was negligible. Duane, however, seemed genuinely refreshed and revitalized. When Phil heard Duane fooling around solo on his guitar one day, he told Duane that he was getting so good it was scaring him. Duane said sometimes he even scared himself. Tom Dowd, the producer, said Duane was getting notes out of his guitar that didn't exist.

After his dismissal from the hospital, Duane stopped in New York to visit friends and then took a flight back to Macon. Everyone was feeling great, and I was delighted to learn that the band was giving my wife Sandra and me an all-expenses paid trip to the Bahamas.

Sandra and I flew to Miami and then on to the Bahamas on Friday afternoon, October 29. We had just checked into the hotel and were dressing for dinner and a night of gambling in the casino when I received a phone call from Bunky Odom at the Walden office. The news was not good. Duane had been involved in a serious motorcycle accident on the way from the Big House to the new house he had rented for himself and his new lady, Dixie. The prognosis was guarded and Duane was in surgery. Bunky would keep me posted. Sandra and I shuffled off to dinner, stunned but hoping for the best. Another call from Bunky interrupted our dinner. Duane had passed on. Howard Duane Allman was born on November 20, 1946. He left us just short of his twenty-fifth birthday.

I was shocked and saddened beyond belief. The real grief came later and remains to this day. I tried to kill the immediate pain by wandering aimlessly from the crap tables to the blackjack tables, but I couldn't concentrate. I ended up in a robotic trance, pulling the handle on a dollar slot machine, before Sandra convinced me to go up to our room. I had to get a grip. There was much to do.

While Bunky Odom was contacting me, Phil Walden's longtime assistant Carolyn Brown was trying to reach him on the nearby island of Bimini. Phil was at dinner too, and communications on Bimini were still somewhat primitive at the time. Eventually, Carolyn reached Phil and arrangements were made for Sandra and me to meet him and his wife Peggy at Miami Airport the next morning. We would fly together to Atlanta and then on to Macon.

Much of the following few days remains a blur in my memory. A local funeral director, Bill Snow of Memorial Chapel, had on his own authority taken custody of Duane's body, and it was agreed to let him handle the services. Arrangements for the Allmans' mother, Geraldine, to travel from Daytona to Macon had to be made. Other friends, family, and music business associates would have to be accommodated as well.

A private service was held on Monday, November 1, 1971, at Memorial Chapel in Macon. The room was jammed when the surviving band members took their places to perform a memorial set for Duane. It was impossible not to feel a sense of joy as the band reeled off some memorable tunes ending with Gregg's solo rendition of "Melissa" and a final band performance of "Statesboro Blues." Then Jerry Wexler of Atlantic Records gave a moving eulogy.

Duane's casket was closed for the service, but it had been kept open in an adjoining room for viewing by immediate family and close friends. It was my job to escort these mourners in and out of the room, and it was tough to maintain my composure in the face of their heartrending and intense expressions of grief. It was one of the hardest things I've ever had to do. Duane was neatly dressed and looked at peace in his silent sleep. Rumors that he was provided a joint in his pocket and a slide bottle on his finger for his final journey are not untrue.

After the service, friends and family scattered to Phil Walden's house, the Big House, and various band members' houses. The mood was somber and many were heavily sedated. Business was not discussed.

17

The Dark Year

I don't believe there was ever the slightest doubt that the band would go forward. There was, of course, the determination to carry on for the sake of Duane and the brotherhood. An economic imperative existed as well. After all, the survivors were professional musicians and would continue to earn a living by writing, recording, and performing. None of us felt that the creative life of the band was over.

Amazingly, we were back at work in New York by mid-November, less than a month after Duane's passing. I will never forget the first gig without Duane's physical presence. It was sad to see his empty spot on the stage, but it was uplifting to see the surviving members carrying on. Our second show was at Carnegie Hall, which would have been a real treat for Duane. We also had killer shows in Boston and Philadelphia with a huge $23,000.00 payday in Philly alone. In Providence, Rhode Island, I would meet a beautiful, intelligent, nineteen-year-old college student with long black hair, dark eyes, and an intense passion for the music of The Allman Brothers Band. Elizabeth LaGrua was from New York City and we eventually had a three-year relationship. Who knew she would come back into my life twenty-five years later and become an integral part in the creation of this book?

We closed out the year back in New Orleans at the Warehouse. Little did we know that the new year would once again bring triumph and tragedy.

Work on the follow-up album to *Live at Fillmore East* had begun prior to Duane's passing, and he performs in the live tracks used from the Fillmore performances as well as in three studio tracks, including the poignant "Little Martha." The album begins, though, with three songs from the five-member band and features Dickey Betts's slide guitar work on "Ain't Wastin' Time No More." I remember Dickey diligently practicing and rehearsing his slide in the studio and at the Thunderbird Hotel, which was our base in Miami for the Criteria Studio sessions. He did an excellent job, but slide work would not become a major part of his recording or performing repertoire. The album, *Eat a Peach*, was released as a two-disc set in February 1972 with beautiful artwork by Jim Flournoy Holmes and W. David Powell of Wonder Graphics. One can gaze for hours at the intricacies of the inner album painting, and the band loved it. Once again, The Allman Brothers

Band had released a critical and commercial smash that would be included on most of the "best of" album lists for 1972.

We continued to crisscross the country with more than sixty dates in the first half of the year. When we took a break mid-year, the band had already grossed more than $800,000.00 from concerts alone. We had sold out performances all over the country, including the major markets of New York, Boston, Philadelphia, Dallas, Houston, Kansas City, Chicago, Atlanta, Denver, San Francisco, and Los Angeles.

Financially, we were doing well. Record royalties that began to come in bolstered the personal appearance income, and the band was able to pay off all debt. Individually, Gregg and Dickey started receiving substantial songwriting royalties from record sales and public performance royalties from Broadcast Music, Inc. I remember riding in a limousine in New York City one afternoon, making a phone call to a childhood friend, Charles Bignon, and asking him to "come help me, we're bigger than Elvis up here." Eventually, my workload became overwhelmingly burdensome, and the band allowed me to hire Charles as a bookkeeper and assistant. He was a great help to me and an asset to the band, and he remains one of my closest friends.

The increasingly bright financial situation led Phil Walden and me to encourage the band to make personal investments. Phil insisted that they not squander all of their earnings. We looked at several opportunities, including a motel priced at $90,000.00, but when the band saw a tract of land just north of Macon in Juliette, Georgia, the die was cast.

The property was truly breathtaking, more than 400 acres of pristine, undeveloped Georgia countryside full of natural beauty and wildlife. It was overpriced at around $150,000.00 as I recall, but the band wanted it and they got it. I used to joke that if the price of something was $150.00, the band would ask the seller if he would take $160.00.

Originally, there were grandiose plans of having our own little city, kind of an "ABB-ville" where everyone would build a home and live. This proved impractical because of trying to subdivide and quit claim out individual plots, as well as the difficulty of reselling individual homes amid the property as a whole. The property was set up as a partnership, Brothers Farms, and operated as a "hobby farm" for tax purposes. At its peak, it drained off about $90,000.00 a year in operating costs, but at least it was tax deductible. For all practical purposes, it became the domain of Dickey, who built a home there, and Butch, who planned but never built one. Years later, it would be sold back to the original owner. Later, the band would also invest in rental apartments and a shopping center.

In April, we performed at a huge outdoor spring break festival in Puerto Rico. The venue was way out in the countryside, and the only transportation for the artists was a small helicopter. By the end of the show, the pilot was exhausted and the helicopter was dangerously overextended. I got some of our traveling party out on his last flight—reluctantly, I might add. For the rest of us, including Gregg, Dickey, and Jaimoe, I had to commandeer a beat-up farm truck complete with farmer, kids, and animals. Gregg sat in the cab and the rest of us sat in the back or hung onto the sides for the long ride back to the hotel. It was quite a sight. So much for economy with dignity.

All was not peaches and cream, however. On the evening of July 21, we performed at a hugely successful outdoor concert in New Orleans presented by the Warehouse promoters, Beaver Productions. After the show, we were settling in at the Marie Antoinette Hotel in the French Quarter when New Orleans police simultaneously smashed in all of our hotel room doors. Busted again, and like last time it was a keystone cops operation with more drugs being missed than discovered. I was not charged, although the police unsuccessfully tried to seize my briefcase that contained more than $35,000.00. I spent the rest of the night bailing out the band, crew, and guests as they were processed one by one. The whole deal didn't pass the smell test. There had been suspicious overtures the night before in Jackson, Mississippi, from some folks wanting to supply party favors for the New Orleans show. The band celebrated that afternoon, I believe, by playing a free concert in the city park. I was on the phone arranging for the services of John Condon.

Mr. Condon visited District Attorney Jim Garrison, of Kennedy assassination conspiracy fame, and noted that his search warrants were faulty. Mr. Garrison eventually concurred, dropping all charges. I believe we did make a political contribution to someone, and rumor has it that some New Orleans police officials were presented with honorary awards, anonymously arranged. I will hereby claim faulty memory on the details.

The New Orleans incident highlighted the ongoing problem of drug use by the band members. Berry Oakley was on a terribly debilitating downward spiral of drug and alcohol abuse. From the beginning, Berry had been the "mother hen" of the group, and I say this with affection. He loved being lord of the manor at the Big House. Poor Berry was now trying to take Duane's place as the spiritual and musical leader of the band, but he simply didn't have the strength for it. On one occasion, he passed out and stopped breathing right in the middle of a conversation with me as he sat on the side of a hotel bed. I quickly summoned Butch Trucks and others and we were able to get him breathing and conscious, walking him back and forth, up and down the hotel corridor. At other times, I would station Tuffy Phillips, our truck driver, on the floor in front of Berry to catch him if he fell off the stage.

It was painful watching Berry deteriorate. While things seemed rosy on the surface, the band itself appeared to be facing personal and creative decline. No one could ever replace Duane, musically or spiritually. The problem was what to do to fill the musical void.

By October, the group began work on yet another album. Gregg also began a solo recording of songs he felt did not quite fit The Allman Brothers Band's style. In retrospect, it's amazing that between July 1969 and June 1973, four long, difficult years, the band completed five all-time classic albums, and Gregg recorded one of his greatest solo efforts. This was an incredible body of work, much of it created under enormous handicaps of personal grief, emotional turmoil, and drug and alcohol abuse.

18

Enter Chuck Leavell

Chuck Leavell, an incredibly talented young keyboardist from Alabama, arrived in Macon initially under the auspices of Capricorn staff producer Paul Hornsby, who had performed with Duane, Gregg, Pete Carr, and Johnny Sandlin in Hour Glass. Paul was producing a band called Sundown for Ampex Records under a releasing arrangement set up by Phil Walden. Chuck recorded and toured with Sundown for about a year until they broke up. Later, he recorded and toured with Capricorn artist Alex Taylor and Phil Walden Management client Dr. John. Both bands frequently opened for The Allman Brothers Band, and Chuck found himself getting into the Brothers' music. He often secretly accompanied the band on his keyboards from a discrete offstage location.

Eventually, these gigs dried up and Chuck returned to Alabama. During summer 1972, Johnny Sandlin invited him back to Macon to perform on Gregg's solo effort, *Laid Back*. Soon, the whole band began showing up in the studio for recording rehearsals, and Chuck became an integral part of their informal jams. This quickly felt right to everyone. The band invited Chuck to play on their new album as well. Chuck recalls Berry Oakley being especially kind to him during this period. Soon thereafter, Phil Walden and the band members reached a decision to invite Chuck to join The Allman Brothers Band. We had a formal meeting in Phil's office on Cotton Avenue. Chuck was pleased and graciously accepted our invitation.

During the same period, discussions began to renegotiate the band's recording agreement with Capricorn. Though some recall it differently, I distinctly remember Phil Walden making the first overtures. The band did have concerns about royalty rates, and one reason was their confusion over rates being based on wholesale or retail. Some artists bragged about getting 14-, 15-, even 20-percent royalties. However, most of these deals were based on wholesale, so the effective rate was about half the contractual rate. The Allman Brothers Band was getting 5 percent of retail or about 10 percent of wholesale, fairly standard for an entry level band, which they were in 1969 when the original contract was signed. Three years later, they could legitimately demand a renegotiated deal based on their success. The deal was in Capricorn's interest as well, for they had just signed on to a new joint venture agreement with Atlantic's corporate parent, Warner Brothers Records. The agreement, dated November 1, 1972, and signed by all five band members, was for one year with four one-year options at the same terms granted to

Capricorn. It provided for royalties of 12 percent of the suggested listed retail price, a signing advance of $100,000.00, and recording budgets of $50,000.00 per album. Any portion of the recording budget not spent would be returned to the band as a further advance, and no charges for studio time used at the Capricorn studios in Macon would accrue to the band. In the future, when the band would tie up the studio for days, weeks, and months, that alone would amount to huge sums. The contract did not specify that the new royalty rate would retroactively apply to earlier recordings, which would later become a sore point for the band.

19

Another Brother Departs

The band's last public performances had been in Atlanta on August 30 and 31, 1972. Since then, they had been involved in rehearsals, preproduction, and recording what would become the *Brothers and Sisters* album and Gregg's *Laid Back*, plus the renegotiation of their recording contract.

In early November, we flew to New York for a television taping of *In Concert*, produced by Don Kirschner for ABC-TV. This would be Chuck Leavell's first official public performance with the band. The taping was completed by mid-afternoon, and by that evening we were back in Macon. By 10:00 PM, I was sitting at the bar at Frank Fenter's new nightclub, the Ad Lib on Cotton Avenue. I remember thinking that this really was the jet age.

Berry Oakley was still walking around loaded most of the time, and he had thrown his efforts almost entirely into a huge jam he was planning called "the jive ass revue, featuring the rowdy roadies and the shady ladies." He was consumed by this project, possibly to prove he could actually be the leader of something positive. It was to take place on Saturday night, November 11, at the Ad Lib.

That afternoon, I had taken a "financial interest" in the outcome of a Georgia Tech football game versus Duke University. I was intently listening to the game unfold on the radio when I received a call that Berry had been in a motorcycle accident and was at the hospital. I walked into the emergency room, encountered Kim Payne, and somewhat jokingly asked what Berry had gotten himself into now. I could immediately tell from Kim's demeanor that this was much more serious than I had been led to believe.

Berry and Kim had been out riding their bikes when Berry had failed to negotiate a curve and slammed into the side of a Macon city bus, eerily near the same area as Duane's accident. He refused to go directly to the hospital and headed back to the Big House. Chuck Leavell recalls arriving there for rehearsals just as Berry walked in from the accident. Shortly thereafter, Berry, who had taken a turn for the worse, was brought downstairs. He was delirious, and everyone piled into Chuck's car and raced to the hospital. Berry did not survive, swiftly succumbing to severe brain injuries.

I can remember my first phone call almost verbatim. It was to Dickey at the farm. I told him, "I've got some bad news. You better sit down. B.O. had an accident on his bike and he didn't make it." Dickey's reaction was shock and disbelief. I'm pretty sure I contacted Gregg as well, who I think was in New York visiting his close friend Deering Howe. That call and other events of the next few days are blurry in my memory. I think most of us were in a foggy state of shock and anguish.

We endured another memorial service, this time at a different location, Hart's Mortuary. Berry's family had also requested a prior service at the Catholic church. The band played again. Chuck recalls Berry's mother asking that "Hootchie Cootchie Man" be played. It was the only song on which Berry ever sang lead for The Allman Brothers Band. The band also performed "Wasted Words" and "In Memory of Elizabeth Reed." Duane Allman and Berry Oakley were together again. Their eternal resting place would be a beautiful and tasteful memorial plot near the Ocmulgee River at Rose Hill Cemetery, a place where they had spent so many spiritual times together only a couple of years before. Along with thousands of other people from all over the world, I visit them there periodically.

Many of us felt like we were actually living and breathing some sort of strange, tragic "Southern Gothic" novel. The unanimous consensus was that nothing would stop us. We were going to play out the hand with whatever cards we were dealt. The band would carry on.

20

The $15,000.00 Line of Cocaine, a Sure Cure for the Hiccups, and Other Promoter Stories

No rock and roll story would be complete without a word about concert promoters. They provide the risk capital for presenting live concert performances. They pay the headline artist and support talent, rent a venue, purchase advertising, provide sound, lighting, and production, hire police and security, arrange catering and local transportation, and do whatever else is necessary to produce a successful event. If the concert is a financial success, promoters earn a profit based on terms negotiated with the artist's management and booking agent. Some promoters have several successful events in a row only to be wiped out by one box office bomb. It is a high-risk business, and only the strong, smart, and well-capitalized promoters survive.

A battle of wits ensues between the artist's representatives and the promoters over finances. There are a myriad of ways for a promoter to pad his expenses, get kickbacks from vendors, and sneak extra ticket sales revenue into his own pocket. From time to time, I used a digital hand clicker provided by Twiggs to count people coming in the door. But that proved impractical at large venues. Turnstile counts at large venues are not reliable either. No amount of diligence on behalf of the artist can completely thwart a crafty promoter, so a sort of live-and-let-live relationship exists between the two sides. The artist's side tries to squeeze every possible nickel into their fee, and the promoter does the same for his bottom line.

Individual promoters and promotion companies had specific cities and regions where they generally controlled the concerts presented in their respective territories. Recent years have seen these territories bought out and controlled by large national promoters like Clear Channel. Some of the old-timers have been employed by their successors. Others have retired or passed on. I had a good relationship with most of the major promoters, but I won't name them because I might leave somebody out. There was a well-known northeastern promoter whose young son supposedly concluded his nightly prayers with "God bless Mommy, Daddy, and The Allman Brothers Band." We probably helped finance his college education.

No discourse on promoters would be complete, however, without mentioning Bill Graham. He was an early and ardent supporter of the band, but negotiations between him and Phil Walden over the band's fees have been referred to in almost mythic terms. It was reportedly a battle between an irresistible force meeting an immovable object, where voices rose and neck veins bulged. I held Bill Graham in awe because of his professionalism, and his shows were always a genuine pleasure to work.

On a lighter note, I recall a story about a promoter ensconced in a hotel room with a lady other than his wife. He had just done a line of cocaine, and, as so often happened, the adulterants in the cocaine caused an immediate laxative effect. Not wanting to use the facilities in the close confines of the hotel room, he briefly excused himself to the lobby with the admonition to his guest not to answer the phone under any circumstances. The phone rang, she answered, and the promoter's wife responded. It took a new Cadillac, costing around $15,000.00 at the time, to square things up with the wife.

On Dickey Betts's first solo tour, I developed a severe case of nervous hiccups due to the stress and anxiety caused by some of Mr. Betts's behavior and general demeanor at the time. I was hiccupping every fifteen to thirty seconds for several days, could not stop, and my stomach muscles ached. A kindly old-school promoter from the Carolinas said he knew a young lady who could surely provide a cure. At his sole expense, she joined the tour and provided delightful companionship to me for a couple of days. My ailment vanished, never to return. If she's still out there, I thank her sincerely.

21

A New Beginning

Before the band could resume touring, they had to hire a new bass player. Several talented players applied for auditions held at the Capricorn studio in Macon. The band selected Lamar Williams, a friend of Jaimoe's from the Gulfport, Mississippi, area. He didn't get the gig just because he was Jaimoe's friend, although that was surely a consideration. He was a damn good bass player, and his style meshed easily with the band.

Lamar had been drafted in the late sixties and eventually shipped out to Vietnam. He was a nonviolent pacifist, and one day when his unit took a column left, Lamar took a column right into the countryside. He was eventually separated from the service and returned to the States. When I put him on the payroll, I discovered he had not filed income tax returns for quite some time, and I had to square him up with the IRS.

The band obviously had dealings with the IRS as well. I scrupulously made sure their business and personal tax returns were filed in an accurate and timely manner through a Macon CPA, Everett Flournoy. I am proud to say that nobody ever had any tax problems on my watch, despite what may have been reported elsewhere.

Tax evasion is a crime; however, tax avoidance is not. With that in mind, a corporation, Brothers Properties, Inc., was formed in early 1973 to shelter income, make investments, and provide tax-free benefits such as pension and profit-sharing plans, medical payments, insurance, and other benefits for the shareholders and employees. The four remaining original band members each had 25-percent ownership of the stock, while Chuck and Lamar were salaried employees. We also eventually rented a small office at 712 Riverside Drive in Macon. Additionally, I took out a large personal surety bond on myself that would reimburse the band for any losses incurred for financial fraud or malfeasance on my part. Again, I'm proud to say no such losses ever occurred on my watch, and no claims were ever filed. The band members had previously operated as an equal partnership. Under Georgia law, a partnership is dissolved upon the death of a partner, so there had been two prior partnerships, now both dissolved.

The first concert with the new lineup was in Ann Arbor at the University of Michigan's indoor hockey arena. Enjoying a phenomenal response, we earned more than $27,000.00. We went on to earn $40,000.00 outdoors on an unseasonably cold, 40-degree night in Hollywood, Florida, and $47,585.00 at the Spectrum in Philadelphia before closing out the year at the Warehouse in New Orleans. Clearly, the public still loved The Allman Brothers Band, and we entered yet another new year with great enthusiasm. Surely fate was smiling on us this time, but one couldn't help feeling some trepidation.

The year 1973 would solidify the band's position among the most successful rock groups in the country. Except for the Warehouse in New Orleans and Bill Graham's Winterland in San Francisco, both of which we played out of loyalty, there were no more club and small hall gigs. It was now arena rock, and soon we would graduate to outdoor stadiums as well. The number of gigs would decrease markedly, as we performed only about fifty concerts over the entire year. The per-show earnings increased tremendously, however, and the gross earnings from concerts alone were more than two and a quarter million dollars.

Around this time, I snorted my first line of cocaine. I never cared much for the effects of marijuana or LSD. Duane had steered me clear of heroin, and I had no real curiosity about cocaine. I didn't want to ingest anything that would hamper my reputation for steel nerves and complete self-control. I did notice many reasonable people using cocaine without any apparent ill effects, though, so one night in a hotel after a concert, I gave in to the insistent demands of our opening act that I join him in a sociable post-gig snort. Amazingly, I discovered no ill affects at all, just a warm feeling of well-being and alertness. With no apologies, I can truthfully say that over the next fifteen years, without a medicinal blast at times of extreme physical and mental fatigue, I wouldn't have been able to get my work done. The social, recreational use and the combination of cocaine and alcohol, however, proved debilitating for me. Thankfully, those times are gone forever.

Recording of the two albums continued simultaneously, and the work progressed much slower than in the past. *Brothers and Sisters* would not be completed and released until July with Gregg's *Laid Back* debuting in October. *Brothers and Sisters* accentuates Dickey's and Chuck's emergence as the musical leaders of the band's new direction. "Jessica" is an instrumental masterpiece, and as I began to hear "Ramblin' Man" over and over on the top-forty radio stations, I slowly realized the band had its first hit single. The song eventually peaked at number two on *Billboard* magazine's chart, while the album reached number one. Gregg's solo effort was a huge success as well. His rendition of Jackson Browne's "These Days" is a classic, as is the remake of "Midnight Rider," and "Queen of Hearts," and "Multi-colored Lady." There is not one throwaway song on the entire album.

Even with all of the critical and financial success, I began to feel a sense of emptiness in the band. The old feelings of brotherhood and camaraderie slowly ebbed away. Chuck, Lamar, and Jaimoe bonded together, but Dickey, Gregg, and Butch were on their own. It was virtually impossible to get all six members together for even the most critical business and career decisions. Increasingly, I would have to make important decisions unilaterally for which I would later be criticized, unjustly in my opinion.

Dickey became the de facto leader of the band. I think even he would agree it was a position for which he was not psychologically equipped. I tried my best to get close to Dickey. There was much to admire about him, and I spent a lot of time helping him with his personal finances, trying to explain the financial mechanics of artist, writer, publisher, and public performance royalties. He was a real chameleon, though, and he would turn from a smiling, friendly, convivial individual into an angry, brooding, violent hellion at the blink of an eye.

The crew had also developed a reputation for surliness. Things got nasty at one of the concerts co-headlined with the Grateful Dead at JFK Stadium in Washington, D.C., on June 9 and 10, 1973. It was hot and stuffy in the jam-packed stadium, and family, friends, executives, celebrities like Caroline Kennedy, and the usual groupies and hangers-on crowded the stage and backstage area. Many of the roadies were roaring on LSD, courtesy of the Dead's crew, and things were tense around the congested stage. The band always ran an open stage filled with family, friends, and hangers-on. I considered it tacky and unprofessional, but the tradition wouldn't die. However, there would come a point at huge events like this when no one else could be allowed on stage. So when Dick Wooley, a Capricorn promotion executive, demanded to be let on stage, an altercation developed. Wooley received a beating and suffered a concussion courtesy of Kim Payne, Tuffy Phillips, and some of the Dead's security. This was the proverbial straw that broke the camel's back. Kim admits that he was taking painkillers for a foot injury and had a bad attitude that day. Phil Walden was outraged that his employee had been assaulted and demanded that something be done. A meeting was held, and it was decided that Kim and Tuffy would be fired because of the fight. Mike Callahan would also be let go because of a similar attitude problem. It was a tough decision for the band, and I had mixed emotions about it. There was no doubt that some of the crew were becoming exceedingly dictatorial and hostile at shows, but that didn't make their firing any more palatable. My separation interviews with Kim, Tuffy, and Mike back in Macon were particularly painful for me.

In another completely unrelated event, Joe Dan Petty later left the crew to form his own band, Grinderswitch.

The Brothers gave him spare equipment, and Grinderswitch opened many shows for us. The band also wanted their own custom sound system, and a subsidiary, Brothers Sound, was formed. Huge new equipment expenditures were made and a large warehouse was rented. All of the new road and sound crew guys were proficient, but they hadn't been there in the lean days, and their sense of loyalty and brotherhood seemed lacking. I know some of them developed a sense of disdain and distrust for the band members, myself, and my staff.

We had received top left billing with the Dead in D.C. It's interesting to note that whenever we co-headlined with bands of equal billing, Phil Walden demanded that the listing be alphabetical. That meant The Allman Brothers Band was always billed top left and first, unless we were ever co-billed with Abba.

A huge highlight that summer was the massive outdoor concert held at the grand prix racetrack in Watkins Glen, New York, on July 28, featuring The Allman Brothers Band, The Band, and The Grateful Dead, billed alphabetically, of course. Advertisements read, "Summer Jam…Come Upstate For A Day Of Music In the Country." The promoters, Shelly Finkel and Jim Koplik, hired Bill Graham to do the production, and he did his usual first-rate job. The sound, lights, and staging were superb, and the backstage area was tastefully landscaped and comfortable. All ingress and egress was by helicopter. The crowds prevented any vehicular movement by the Thursday preceding Saturday's concert.

Sound checks for each band were scheduled for Thursday, but rain delayed them until Friday. By that time, more than 150,000 fans waited excitedly. Only 150,000 attendees had been expected for the entire event. The gates were opened early on Friday, and Graham asked the bands to perform their sound checks in front of the gathering throng. Each band performed for a couple of hours as a preview of the real concert scheduled twenty-four hours later. This was a great idea that kept the crowd in a friendly mood. By Saturday, the crowd grew to an estimated 600,000, a number memorialized in the Guinness Book of World Records. The concert went off without a hitch for a mellow, appreciative, and well-behaved crowd. Only one death, an unfortunate skydiving accident, occurred.

I had never seen so many people. It was incredible. The roads were filled with an unending stream of humanity. It reminded me of what the end of the world or the aftermath of a nuclear attack might look like. The only flaw was that the crowds overwhelmed any orderly effort to continue selling tickets. Peaceful but massive gate crashing occurred, and the promoters had no choice but to make it a free event. Even so, enough sales had been made so that the event was a financial success.

Each band had agreed to receive a flat fee of $117,500.00 under a "most favored nations" policy of identical fees and perks. Phil Walden recognized immediately that it was appropriate to demand more based on the receipts taken in when ticket sales stopped. He huddled in a car with the promoters and negotiated an additional $75,000.00 for The Allman Brothers Band on the spot. In November, after all accounting had been done, we received another $11,136.00. Apparently, none of the other bands' representatives were as perceptive. Years later, I ran into an attorney for one of them and he was nonplussed but not surprised that Phil Walden had out-negotiated him.

In November, the band insisted on chartering the Starship for their touring. It was a full-sized Boeing 720 airliner converted to limited seating and luxury appointments, including a huge bar, video cassette players (new at the time), and a bedroom with a faux fireplace. Deep Purple, The Moody Blues, Bob Dylan, The Beach Boys, Led Zeppelin, Alice Cooper, John Denver, and Vegas high roller junketeers were among those who used it. The flight attendants stocked up on soul food from our favorite local restaurant, Mama Louise's H and H. Needless to say, my economy with dignity policy was now out the window. I also became enamored with one of the Starship's beautiful California flight attendants, Suzanne Carnel. We had a brief romance and then established a long, ongoing friendship. Initially, though, it was one of the many causes of the breakup of my marriage to Sandra.

We ended our year for Bill Graham at the Cow Palace in San Francisco. The New Year's Eve concert was broadcast coast to coast on a network of radio stations set up by Capricorn Records. We did multiple countdowns of the new year for each time zone, and Bill Graham descended from the ceiling dressed in diapers as Baby 1974 when midnight struck on the west coast. We had made it through the year without a major tragedy.

22

Wives, Girlfriends, Groupies, and Band Aids

At one time or another, all of the band members from my era had at least one marriage. Of the surviving members, only Chuck and Rose Lane Leavell have avoided divorce. In a country with a 50-percent divorce rate, rock and roll marriages, like Hollywood marriages, face the extra handicaps of frequent temptations and geographical separation. The seventies were not that far removed from the sexual liberation of the sixties, and frequent, willing partners abounded. Also, the consequences of the most common sexually transmitted diseases were a few days of discomfort and were easily overcome with simple antibiotics.

We worked hard, traveled continuously, and, as mentioned, met many willing partners. There was little time for wooing with gifts of candy, flowers, or cards. I called it "nontraditional courtship." One availed himself of the opposite sex whenever, wherever, and however conditions permitted.

Some of us had more or less regular girlfriends in some cities whom we saw on every visit and for whom we had real feelings of affection. Mutual faithfulness and wives at home were not discussed. There were also the groupies, girls who always showed up in their respective cities and provided sexual favors to one or more members of the group. Some would even help with laundry, sewing, or other mundane necessities of the road. Most were sweet, kind, and sincere. Others obviously sought only drugs, partying, and the vicarious thrill of being "with the band." You knew they would transfer their affection to almost each and every band that came through their town. Of the later group, some were what I called "band aids." They were faces without names that often showed up at the venue early in the afternoon bestowing their sexual favors on the road crew in exchange for a backstage pass and a chance to hook up with a band member later at the show. They would also cluster around the stage during the show, at the stage door before and after the show, and in the hotel lobby and bar at the end of the evening. It was a strange, sad, and somewhat demeaning aspect of rock and roll life.

Once in Memphis, we had just checked into a hotel when the road crew excitedly alerted us to a beautiful young lady who was making her sexual favors available to everyone. She looked like a model who had stepped from the pages of *Seventeen* magazine. Supposedly, her mother had brought her to Memphis for a weekend shopping trip to keep her away from trouble back home in Little Rock. Her name was Connie; she was later dubbed Sweet Connie and memorialized in song by Grand Funk Railroad and in the pages of numerous magazine articles. For better or worse, we were her first band. I last saw Connie in the mid-eighties when The Gregg Allman Band passed through Little Rock. She had become a schoolteacher but was still sweet and still sexually talented.

On an earlier occasion, one of the band's favorite ladies from Atlanta met an untimely death from an accidental drug overdose. Berry Oakley instructed me to buy every fresh rose in the city of Atlanta to cover her coffin. I complied as best I could. She had been my first sexual partner on the road.

23

The Pinnacle

For the first time since its inception in 1969, The Allman Brothers Band did not record as a group in 1974. Dickey recorded his first solo effort, *Highway Call*, between March and June for release in July. Dickey's recording would provide my first meeting with a Beatle. I literally ran into John Lennon, almost knocking him down as he entered and I exited the Record Plant in New York where Dickey's album was being mixed. In addition, a live album with lots of studio overdubs was culled from Gregg's spring solo tour and released in August.

Frank Fenter and Phil Walden had always told us that the band's first two albums would start selling again based on the sales of the later recordings and the band's phenomenal touring success. With that in mind, those first two albums were repackaged and re-released in April 1974 as a double album set titled *Beginnings*. It soon earned a gold record award.

When most bands are off the road and not touring, key support personnel are often put on a retainer to insure their services for later tours. The Allman Brothers Band kept every member of the band and crew on full salary permanently. While generous and benevolent, with the weekly payroll at around $10,000.00, it was financially extravagant. The band did not tour again until June 1974.

First, Gregg Allman mounted a solo tour in support of his *Laid Back* album. We did approximately thirty shows in thirty-nine days. Highlights included the Fox Theater in Atlanta, the Music Hall in Boston, and Carnegie Hall in New York. Chuck Leavell and Jaimoe headed a seven-piece rhythm section that also featured Scott Boyer and Tommy Talton of Cowboy, a Capricorn band. Randall Bramblett led a five-piece horn section. A venerable old New York string master, Max Kahn, supervised a large string section, and, finally, there were three female background singers. Ed Freeman arranged and conducted this impressive orchestra. Johnny Sandlin was musical director. Larry Hitchcock and Joe Gannon, who had produced Alice Cooper's great stage show, provided first-rate staging and lighting. After getting a few kinks out of the sound system, the shows fully captured the sound of the *Laid Back* album, and the tour was a creative and financial success.

The touring logistics were difficult but went well. Gregg and I, plus one or two rotating guest passengers, traveled on a small single-engine plane. The rest of the band and crew traveled on a Trailways charter bus, all seats and no bunks. That was tough on some of the long jumps, and there were always frantic negotiations and jockeying to get on the plane with Gregg. Twiggs overcame his personal sleeping discomfort on the bus by bunking in the overhead luggage rack. Twiggs, Red Dog, and Larry Brantley handled the stage flawlessly, and once the aforementioned kinks were worked out, Brothers Sound, headed by Buddy Thornton, did a great job. I also had major help from Charles Bignon, Bunky Odom, and Buffalo Evans. There was little time to rest on our laurels, though. The biggest tour in Allman Brothers history would begin in a month.

The tour was billed as "Summer Campaign '74," and the souvenir program featured an American eagle and General Robert E. Lee on his horse Traveller bursting through the Confederate battle flag. This was a more innocent time before the stars and bars were largely taken over by racists and skinheads. The Allman Brothers Band had a true Southern heritage, but it had nothing to do with racism. I did, however, kid the Northern promoters' accountants that we were there to avenge Sherman's march through Georgia and that I was taking all the Yankee money back home.

We worked only large arenas and outdoor stadiums. In June alone, the band grossed an incredible $1,088,364.04 from only nine cities. This included the show at Atlanta Stadium mentioned in an earlier chapter. We earned our biggest fee ever, but barely. For some unfathomable reason, the promoters built an uncovered stage, and early showers threatened to wash out the whole concert. By mid-afternoon, the sun was out, all the opening bands had played, and the weather was no longer a concern. All problems were over, I thought, as we settled into our dressing rooms in the bowels of the huge stadium. More than 60,000 excited fans would soon enjoy their heroes. Then disaster struck. Someone had deliberately dosed Lamar and accidentally dosed Gregg and Jaimoe with a powerful drug that we later determined to be an animal tranquilizer. We had a hanger-on who had been angling for Lamar's bass guitar gig, and he was a major suspect, but we never conclusively pinpointed him as the culprit. The problem at hand was playing the show. We took everyone to an emergency medical facility on site to survey the damage. Lamar was unable to count the fingers in front of his face, and there was no way he could perform. We recruited Joe Dan Petty to sit in on bass, led Gregg and Jaimoe to their instruments, and plunged ahead. After the usual mid-set break, Lamar was able to take over for Joe Dan, and the show finished without further incident.

Also, just prior to our performance, sound crew member Michael Artz had been detained by police for wearing a knife that violated an Atlanta blade length law. Twiggs and about seventeen other crewmen showed up with identical knives, demanding that they all be arrested and the show would not continue. The police thought better of that and released Artz.

I did not consider this one of the band's more stellar performances and cringed when I saw a major writer for *Rolling Stone* magazine and the *Atlanta Journal* newspaper furiously scribbling on his notepad. His review, published later, was glowing. I was glad to get the payoff and get the hell out of there. We would have further cliffhangers throughout the summer, including temporarily losing Gregg in Amsterdam, Holland. He vanished with one of the Doobie Brothers, but Scooter Herring eventually rounded him up. Gregg also experienced an almost fatal overdose in New York City. Scooter and I, thankfully, were able to resuscitate him before medical help arrived. I now had John "Scooter" Herring on the payroll officially as an advance man and security director.

The band could still deliver amazing, masterful sets, and fans went home deliriously happy. Behind the scenes, however, most of us realized the creative fire was dwindling and the warm feelings of brotherhood and camaraderie were all but gone. We were basically just grinding it out, making and spending huge sums of money. The Starship sometimes idled for hours at the small Macon airport waiting for Gregg to arrive. Initially, no facilities existed for restarting its engines if they were shut down. Each band member had huge hotel suites, and Gregg, Dickey, and Butch kept a personal limo on-call virtually around the clock. Drug and alcohol abuse was more out of control than ever. There seemed to be no long-term solution for these problems. The best I could do was try to minimize the daily horrors I witnessed. While I was certainly no paragon of virtue, I did try to maintain a modicum of self-control in order to keep the wheels from coming off the entire enterprise. Thankfully, we finished in late August and headed home to Georgia. The souvenir program cover proved prophetic as I felt like I had fought and survived on the losing side of a major war.

Both Gregg's live album from the spring tour and Dickey's solo effort were released that summer, so it was decided that they would close out the year with simultaneous solo tours to promote their albums. Also, Gregg would hit additional markets that his successful spring tour had missed. Two things were certain. First, the allocation of resources and personnel would have to be handled judiciously to deal with two delicate egos, and the natural rivalry that had evolved between Gregg and Dickey. Second, I couldn't road manage two tours simultaneously. While both tours would be difficult, it was deemed that Dickey's might prove to be the more difficult of the two, so I took that assignment. Scooter Herring road managed Gregg's tour, and Hewell "Chank" Middleton, Gregg's longtime friend, went along as Gregg's personal assistant. I had given Scooter a crash course in road managing, and he had worked closely with me during the band's summer tour, so I was somewhat confident that he could handle it. He acquitted himself reasonably well for a rookie, and the slimmed-down encore version of Gregg's solo tour played off without major problems.

From the beginning, it was obvious that Dickey felt like he had gotten the short end of the stick. Gregg had most of the A-team production crew and Brothers Sound. Dickey had most of the players from his *Highway Call* album, including fiddler Vassar Clements, The Poindexters (a bluegrass band), a horn section, and three female background singers. He did not have the services of Chuck Leavell, Lamar Williams, and Jaimoe, who went with Gregg, or Butch Trucks, who stayed home.

Dickey, who at the time preferred to be called Richard professionally, had designed the show as a showcase for the influence of country music on modern rock and roll. His ambitious undertaking never quite jelled. The tour had a huge overhead and did not do great business. The album, while successful, did not approach the sales of Gregg's *Laid Back* studio album, which went gold. Dickey had insisted the tour be billed as Richard Betts, an American Music Show. To this day, I believe some fans didn't realize that this was a rock concert featuring Dickey Betts of The Allman Brothers Band, although it was heavily advertised and promoted.

Things got off to an unceremonious start when Dickey's tour bus showed up in a filthy and bedraggled condition. My secretary Jana Vickers and I orchestrated a frantic cleanup, but Dickey was still not happy. I wasn't satisfied either, so we fired the bus company and hired a quick replacement. Also, early in the tour I was called to a hotel lobby where a combative Mr. Betts was creating a disturbance, trying to break through the oak doors of the now-closed motel bar he had visited earlier. He was in a full karate attack posture and was not to be trifled with. I was certainly no match for Dickey, but, amazingly, I was able to apply a headlock and hold on for dear life. I believe it was tour advance man Buffalo Evans who came to my assistance. Between the two of us, we were able to get Dickey to his room and into bed. But the pressure of Dickey's head against my jaw had cracked one of my teeth, and it was not long before I developed my major attack of acute nervous hiccups.

We stumbled along to mediocre business, and Dickey's disposition did not improve. Some of the backup musicians were also drinking and doping heavily, and one of the female background singers had to be fired and sent home. Dickey had wanted to charter a private railroad car for the jump from Chicago to the West Coast, and I obliged. The whole entourage left Chicago on a Friday afternoon, arriving in Los Angeles on Sunday morning. It was an enjoyable and nostalgic respite, but the tour bus scheduled to meet the train to drive us to San Diego did not show up, necessitating a frantic last-minute search for alternate transportation. Dickey wasn't there to complain. He had gotten off the train in New Mexico, hooking up with some Indian medicine men to procure peyote for religious ceremonial purposes. I was able to fly him in to San Diego just in time for the concert. I had already temporarily lost the service of advance man Buffalo Evans, who vanished for days with film actress Elizabeth Ashley. Buffalo did set me up with a beautiful New York model by the name of Heidi, so I forgave him. I spent many late nights commiserating over the phone with Scooter about our mutual tour problems, but finally it was over. We all needed a break and a rest, and we would certainly get one. The Allman Brothers Band wouldn't work again until August 31, 1975.

24

Charities and Benefits

The Allman Brothers Band had been generous and charitable since its inception. The ability to raise money through their concerts proved helpful to a number of causes through the years. Just after I was hired, we performed a benefit in Jacksonville for a terminally ill young girl. This was primarily at the behest of Berry and Butch, as I recall. Later, when Duane accepted a key to the city on behalf of the band from the straitlaced mayor of Jacksonville, I advised Duane, perhaps irreverently, that it was probably the backdoor key.

The Bibb County jail in Macon was a hellhole, and even though a few television sets had been approved for the corridor outside the cell block, there was no money in the budget to purchase them. The band picked up the tab. Later, they did a benefit in Macon that raised huge sums for various local charities and agencies. Often, too, they would donate autographed albums, guitars, or memorabilia for auction at charitable events.

Even though the band was primarily apolitical, there was some rapport with the Democratic governor of Georgia at the time, former President Jimmy Carter. Carter was a new progressive governor, and he had a genuine interest in the band's music. Phil Walden had brought him down to the Capricorn studios, where he spent time with Dickey. Gregg was later invited to the Governor's Mansion where, typically, he showed up late in the middle of the night. Carter got out of bed to meet him, and they hit it off immediately. Most Democratic figures scoffed at the Carter presidential campaign, and he needed money early on to run a meaningful primary campaign. At Phil Walden's request, the band performed a benefit for Carter in Providence, Rhode Island, on November 25, 1975, that is generally recognized as keeping Carter in the race at that point. Other Capricorn acts would later perform benefits as well. We all had to have background checks from the Secret Service, and I made sure their detail at the concert meshed well with our crew. Later, I wrote a note to the head of the Secret Service at the Treasury Department thanking him for the courtesy and cooperation of his agents at this event. He wrote me back saying my note marked the first time in the history of the agency that they had ever gotten a thank-you for their service from any member of the public.

Later, when Carter was the nominee, the opposition party saw a chance to besmirch him because of his association with a bunch of drugged-out hippie musicians. Carter's answer was basically that he liked the music and accepted the people who made it regardless of their foibles. Phil Walden tells of hearing from Macon's Republican mayor, "Machine Gun" Ronnie Thompson, who told him of a meeting he attended in which party leaders discussed plans to smear Carter over his association with Walden and The Allman Brothers Band. The same suspicion of Republican "dirty tricks" later popped up again during the investigation of Scooter Herring's drug dealings with Gregg. Politics, as they say, is not beanbag. Carter, of course, was subsequently elected in a close race with Gerald Ford. Even though the band had broken up by 1977, they performed individually at the inauguration, and some of us attended other events at the White House.

Dickey had always been somewhat of an outdoorsman, and his marriage to a Canadian Native Indian, Sandy Bluesky, had enlightened him to the plight of Native Americans. We set up, at Dickey's request, the North American Indian Foundation as a nonprofit organization to fund Indian cultural heritage projects, hiring a young law student, Steve Massarsky, to run the day-to-day activities. As I recall, the band performed a couple of benefit concerts in Los Angeles and Boston to fund the foundation. Later, Phil Walden, Frank Fenter, Twiggs,

Scooter, and I went with Dickey to Banff, Alberta, Canada, north of Calgary, to discuss disbursement of the funds for various projects. It was scenic country, and the traditional ceremonies were beautiful and moving. Being a tenderfoot city boy, I prepared to rough it overnight under the stars. When I inquired as to the whereabouts of Dickey's tribal leader friends, imagine my surprise to learn that they had all headed back to town to the comforts of the local Holiday Inn.

25

Trouble in the Studio and a National Soap Opera

Recording of the band's first studio album in almost two years began in early 1975. The resultant product was completed and released as *Win, Lose, or Draw* in August. It was not a happy process, and the final results showed it. You could count on Chuck, Lamar, and usually Jaimoe to show up for sessions, but Dickey, Gregg, and Butch only appeared sporadically. I can recall walking into the studio some evenings and finding Johnny Sandlin and his assistants sitting there forlornly waiting for someone to show up. Johnny and drummer Bill Stewart eventually played drums on some tracks. The album offers a few decent songs, but most of it is uninspired and ultimately disappointing. Indeed, the most creative aspect of the entire project was Twiggs's cover design of each band member's profile silhouetted in the playing card border, which many fans were never even aware of. The album sold well enough to earn a gold record award, but sales were down and there were many returns.

I spent a lot of time cleaning up Butch's and Dickey's scrapes with the law—driving under the influence, drunk and disorderlies, and car wrecks. One somewhat humorous incident involved Dickey attacking his wife Sandy Bluesky's unoccupied Mercedes with an axe after one of their numerous violent arguments. The insurance adjustor was not amused. Local law enforcement officers gave us a wide berth, but sometimes they had to haul the boys in. On another occasion, the Macon Police Department called me to come get Dickey and singer-songwriter Billy Joe Shaver out of jail. They had been arrested for public drunkenness, I believe, but they were being so disruptive in jail, disturbing police and prisoners alike, that I was asked to bail them out and take them elsewhere. Conversely, when Jaimoe was brought up on minor traffic charges in state court, he complicated matters by requesting to pay a partial fine and serve jail time to get some rest. Charles Bignon quickly paid the fine in cash and hustled Jaimoe out of court.

Gregg had been spending a lot of time in Los Angeles accompanied by longtime friend and sometime personal assistant Hewell "Chank" Middleton. I was grooming Scooter Herring for more office and tour management responsibilities, and Chank had pretty much taken on the day-to-day responsibilities of keeping up with Gregg. On one of their visits, Gregg and Cher met. They both agreed their first date was a disaster, but they tried again. After a whirlwind, on again/off again courtship, everyone was surprised when they married in Las Vegas early that summer. We were further surprised to learn of a huge argument during their honeymoon in Jamaica. Gregg was missing and had reportedly been seen leaving a bar with two locals and vanishing into the tropical night. I had visions of a drug deal gone bad and Gregg being found dead from machete wounds in a cane field. Chank, Scooter, and I went on full battle alert. Somehow, Gregg got himself to Miami and, broke and disheveled, managed to call and ask us to fly him home.

A few days later, I got a call from a reporter at the *Macon Telegraph* newspaper asking for a comment on Cher's announcement that she was filing for divorce from Gregg. I initially denied the story because no one connected with the band or the Walden office knew anything about it. Within minutes, though, we did confirm it. Shortly thereafter, we had Gregg back in a drug detoxification and treatment program in Buffalo, New York. Cher soon appeared at his side for an attempted reconciliation, and the divorce action was dropped. Dickey's troubled marriage to Sandy Bluesky ended in divorce during this period, and he later married and divorced Cher's personal assistant, Paulette Eghazarian.

By late summer, we were ready to tour again. Gregg, Chuck, Scooter, and I joined Phil Walden, Frank Fenter, and Bunky Odom for a luncheon at New York City's 21 Club to sign contracts for the first rock concert to be held during opening week of the brand new New Orleans Superdome. The place was so cavernous that we actually had to use a limo to transport Gregg and Cher from the dressing room to the stage. Dickey and Paulette may have been in the limo too, but everyone else traveled to the stage in golf carts, I believe. We received a $125,000.00 guarantee and an overage of almost $45,000.00, but things didn't smell right. We had strong suspicions of hanky panky, and there were eyewitness accounts of special ticket deals that didn't show up in the settlement. A civil lawsuit was filed on behalf of the band charging fraud, but we did not prevail in court.

I called this the "brother-in-law" tour because, figuratively, everybody and their brothers-in-law were hired. Scott Hayes recalls me telling him it was likely to be the last tour, and he might as well come on board too. Scott's official title, along with former Otis Redding road manager Earl "Speedo" Simms, was advance man. That job consisted of traveling ahead of the band to pre-register us at hotels, make room assignments, meet the charter flight with limos and room keys, and have the bellmen distribute our numerically coded luggage. They would load and dispatch limos to and from the gigs and then, finally, fly commercial to the next city. I often assigned Scott to help with security for Gregg and Cher as well. He was proficient at keeping pesky tabloid reporters and photographers at bay. Charles Bignon, Jana Vickers, and Buffalo Evans assisted me at the home office and on the road. Scooter Herring was the overall director of security. Chank was Gregg's personal assistant again, and Dickey's longtime friend Buddy Yochim assisted him. Red Dog, Twiggs, and Larry Brantley ran the stage. Buddy Thornton and a crew of three ran sound, and Twigg's brother Andy called lights. We also had truck drivers headed by Buddy's brother Sid Yochim, a lighting crew, two pilots, and one flight attendant. Could we have gotten by with less? The answer, of course, is yes. Did the band approve all of this? The answer, again, is also yes.

The Gregg and Cher saga was outrageous. They had turned into a national soap opera, and most of the publicity was not favorable to them. *People* magazine did what was supposed to be a profile on the band, but it turned out to be a Gregg and Cher story with the rest of the band almost an afterthought. I remember it hitting the newsstands around our second tour date in Oklahoma and how it disappointed most of the band. For the record, I always found Cher to be kind, thoughtful, and charming. She never asked for special treatment. I think, up to that time, she was Gregg's one true love in life, but neither of them was able to handle the incredible internal and external pressures their marriage faced.

Something else happened beginning on our second date in Oklahoma. We didn't go into overage percentage there or on the next two shows. Things improved and attendance rose as we headed back to the northeast, but it was beginning to look and feel as if some of the bloom was off the rose. I had gotten angry with Dickey and Gregg over some now long-forgotten grievance on a five-day break between Atlanta and Phoenix. I semi-threatened to quit and didn't show up in Phoenix until the show was already under way. It was perhaps a portent of things to come.

Attendance was down on the west coast as well. We didn't go into overage percentage on any of the shows, except for Oakland. One show for Bill Graham in Bakersfield was a financial disaster. Also, Jaimoe, who had a history of back problems, developed serious muscle spasms, and a knot the size of a melon popped up on his back. Later, he required a personal physical therapist to travel with him, and we added Bill Stewart as a reserve drummer. At the Los Angeles show at the Forum, two young aspiring and relatively unknown actors named Nick Nolte and Don Johnson were our guests. We had met them earlier when they were filming a low-budget movie, *Return to Macon County*, near the farm back in Macon. I had been collecting vintage cars, and I rented several from the fifties to the production and actually drove as an extra in some scenes that mostly ended up on the cutting room floor. Later, Don Johnson would write with the band and record with Gregg on his solo *I'm No Angel* album. At the same show, the band had asked me to hold one of the dressing room doors shut while they did a blast of coke. Someone kept pushing the door to get in, and finally I flung it open, yelling, "Who the f--- are you and what the f--- do you want?" The guy politely explained that he was Bruce Springsteen and he had been invited. I told him to come in. I think this was around the time when he graced the covers of *Time* and *Newsweek* magazines.

We finished the year with sixteen more shows back east, ending up in Lakeland, Florida, on New Year's Eve. I was miserable with the way things were going and had begun to booze it up both on and off the road. I had also begun to get information that the Federal Government was taking an interest in the band's drug use back in Macon, specifically as it related to Gregg's involvement with a local pharmacist and how he had met him through Scooter Herring.

26

The Beginning of the End

I don't think any of us knew exactly what the feds were up to. We made what I now know to have been a strategic error by retaining a local attorney for Gregg. He did what any attorney would do, which was to look out for the best interests of his client. That would not turn out to be in the best interests of others. Perhaps too late, we sent for the heavy artillery from Buffalo. They had saved us many times before. Could they do it again?

In early January, we were back on the road when we received word that several of us were subpoenaed to appear before a federal grand jury in Macon the next day. We asked for a postponement but were denied. Our new smaller and less expensive tour plane was a turbo prop and likely wouldn't get us back to Macon after the evening's show in time for an early morning appearance, so we chartered a Lear. Upon arrival, Macon was fogged in so we diverted to Atlanta, which was also fogged in. Finally, though, we were able to land at another smaller field on the west side of Atlanta where limos waited to drive us down to Macon. Imagine the financial expense.

We were not in the best condition to be grilled by a federal attorney in a closed grand jury proceeding where our own attorneys were not allowed. I did follow legal advice and told the prosecutor I refused to answer any questions based on my rights under not only the Fifth Amendment, but also the First, Fourth, Sixth, and Ninth. Based on that, he didn't even call me into the grand jury room to go through the motions. I'd like to think my personal code of honor of D&D (deaf and dumb) regarding information on a friend would have held up under any pressure from the government. In my heart, I know I was just stubborn and hardheaded enough to stick to that, but one really never knows how one will react until he is faced with the full force and power of the federal government. For now, things seemed under control and any problems would be faced later.

We jetted right back to the tour like nothing had happened. Things were happening, though. They were actually getting worse. Based on the fall business, our guaranteed concert fees were far below previous highs, and the overage percentages got smaller and happened more rarely. We simply couldn't sustain our ongoing expenses based on the current reduced earnings. The band's huge personal and tour spending habits and their bloated overhead had finally outpaced their ability to earn. Our cash reserves were dwindling fast.

After a show in Columbia, South Carolina, on January 24, we didn't work again until the Kentucky Derby on April 30. Then we performed two miserable shows in Knoxville and Roanoke, and that was it. Around the first of June, almost exactly six years to the day since I started work, I voluntarily tendered my letter of resignation. I was not fired or asked to resign. I chose to leave on my own volition. The main reason was my utter disgust at seeing the band coming apart at the seams. Secretly, I hoped I might shock them into getting back on track. Days after I dropped my bombshell, Scooter Herring also resigned, saying that if conditions were bad enough to cause me to leave, he couldn't continue either. An even bigger bombshell would soon follow.

27

The Real Scooter Herring Story

John C. "Scooter" Herring recalls meeting Gregg Allman and pharmacist Joe Fuchs at about the same time. He had been spending long hours and working late into the night painting a Corvette for Fuchs. Fuchs offered speed to help Scooter stay awake. Scooter mentioned that his wife enjoyed Quaaludes, and Fuchs provided them as well. At first the drugs were free, but later Fuchs charged a nominal fee.

Scooter soon found himself enjoying the Quaaludes, too. One day, Gregg noticed Scooter staggering around the Sunshine Club, a local bar and hangout, and asked if he could have some of whatever Scooter was enjoying. Scooter obliged. Of course, Gregg wanted more and soon provided Scooter with a virtual wish list of his wants. Most were injectable downers, but when Gregg discovered Scooter had access to pharmaceutical cocaine, he wanted some of that too. Unbeknownst to Gregg, Scooter and Fuchs entered into an enterprise to partially supply Gregg's almost insatiable drug habit. Based on Fuchs's knowledge, they attempted to keep the quantities and dosages at nonlethal levels. At some point, Gregg saw Scooter standing behind the counter at Fuchs's drugstore and reportedly asked him how he'd gotten a backstage pass. Fuchs's cover was blown, but after initially worrying about it, he became one of Gregg's biggest groupies. Gregg now got his drugs directly from the source, and Scooter was no longer needed to mediate. If there was a positive side to this sordid mess, it was the thought that the arrangement might help keep Gregg from trying to score even more dangerous street dope on his own...maybe.

I first heard about Scooter from some of the band and crew; he was a former drug supplier who now wanted to try to help Gregg. It was suggested that it might be a good idea to hire Scooter to help take care of Gregg and be a general gopher. I hated injectable drugs and the people who sold them, but Scooter appeared sincerely contrite and eager to help. I agreed to have a meeting with him, and I perceived him as a sincere but obviously rogue outlaw. We were all outlaws, though, and if you don't know the difference between an outlaw and a crook, read some Tom Robbins books. After our meeting, I jokingly told Scooter that my plan was either to hire him or have him done away with. With the band's approval, Scooter was hired. He was not hired to be Gregg's dope procurer. He was hired as Gregg's personal assistant and watchdog, and if he did well, he could expect more responsibilities in the future. He was also encouraged to try to keep Gregg away from needles, and he did try. Scooter was certainly not drug-free himself at the time, but neither was anyone else in our organization. He seemed genuinely excited, though, about the opportunity to put his former lifestyle behind him.

Scooter took on his new responsibilities with enthusiasm and was a great help to me. Discounting the drug use, keeping Gregg satisfied was no day at the beach. He often stayed up for days at a time, and there were always wives and girlfriends to deal with. Gregg liked to delegate his dirty work to others. I remember checking into Miami's Sheraton Four Towers hotel once, and by the end of our time there Gregg had a woman in each of the four towers. The logistics on his girlfriends alone was maddening and almost a full-time job.

Once at a Holiday Inn in the northeast, Gregg was handling a gun in Scooter's room. As Scooter warned him to stop, Gregg said those famous words, "It's not loaded," just as the gun discharged. Scooter told an ashen-faced Gregg to go straight to his room, get under the bed, and stay there. Scooter called to tell me what happened and said he would stand still for it. He then called the front desk and told them his gun had gone off as he was cleaning it and they had better check the adjoining room. Hotel security and police swarmed

Scooter's room almost immediately. The shot had gone through the wall with the spent bullet landing in the bed next door. Luckily, the unhurt but shaken occupant had been in the bathroom. Scooter was whisked off to jail before I could get downstairs, so I jumped into a cab in front of the hotel and demanded to be rushed to police headquarters. The driver made a U-turn and delivered me directly across the street to the jail. Scooter was quickly bailed out, and the authorities dropped charges of unlawful possession of a firearm, although they kept the gun, a short-barrel .38. The front page of the morning paper featured a story headlined "Shot Rocks Holiday Inn," and the congenial police officers were our VIP guests at that evening's performance. This time, we didn't have to call attorney John Condon.

Scooter and I didn't serve Gregg alone. In many instances, the others could be just as demanding and aggravating. Once, Dickey had Scooter and me tracking his estranged wife, Sandy Bluesky. He did not want her to take their young daughter Jessica out of the country to Sandy's home in Canada. We had been on the case for days, tracking Sandy from motels to friends' houses, and were always a step behind her. Finally, we caught up with her in the Atlanta airport and, as I shadowed Sandy through the Eastern Airlines concourse, I dispatched Scooter to look for the child with her grandmother perhaps trailing behind. Sandy never saw me and boarded her flight alone. Meanwhile, Scooter attempted to snatch a small child away from a grandmotherly type in a case of mistaken identify. We were both lucky not to have been arrested for attempted kidnapping. The real child and grandmother had left the country days earlier. Oh well, another day at the office.

I became very close to Scooter. I admired and respected his dedication to his work, his basic intelligence, and his loyalty. Loyalty is important to me. I try to give it unconditionally, and I expect it from others. I sincerely believed Scooter was trying to overcome his past failures and weaknesses. When the chips were down, he never failed to deliver.

The feds frequently make their arrests on Friday afternoon. It's difficult for the accused to connect with an attorney or get a quick bail hearing, so one usually has to stew in jail all weekend, basically incommunicado. After lunch on the Friday before Memorial Day 1976, Scooter was arrested at the band office on Riverside Drive. He was handed five felony drug charges worth seventy-five years in prison. Since Monday was a federal holiday, he would have an additional day to think about what to do.

The star witnesses against Scooter were Gregg Allman and Joe Fuchs. Gregg was given immunity, and Fuchs made a plea agreement for his testimony against Scooter and others in an unrelated trial. Scooter refused to accept a plea agreement in return for his testimony relating to Gregg and in the other matter (the trial involving alleged local organized crime figures). It didn't sink in at the moment, but it was obvious Scooter's goose was cooked. Since Gregg would be testifying against Scooter, the Condon law firm had a conflict of interest. They were not representing Gregg in the current case, but they had represented him in the past and could not ethically represent Scooter. They did recommend a talented young lawyer from Buffalo named Thomas Santa Lucia. He and Burl Davis, a local attorney, would represent Scooter.

Even though I had resigned my position with the band, I was still officially the trustee of their pension and profit-sharing plans. While the band's corporate accounts had been drastically reduced, large balances remained in the retirement accounts, and the plans would have to be liquidated and paid out to each individual member of the band and crew if Brothers Properties, Inc., ceased operations. Also, Charles Bignon was still the band's bookkeeper and held the checkbooks, so I gave him unofficial and off-the-record guidance. Fast-breaking events had made the unofficial breakup of the band official, public, and nasty.

28

The Scooter Herring Trial and Beyond

There was an almost universally virulent reaction toward Gregg. Most of his bandmates expressed their utter disgust for him. They said they would never work with him again. The band was finished. In all fairness to Gregg, there wasn't much he could do to save Scooter. Also, the feds can put the fear of God into almost anyone. Few can stand up to the government's threats. Gregg Allman was not among those few.

The case against Scooter was cut and dried. One hoped for a recalcitrant juror to hold out and cause a mistrial or perhaps a conservative judge who would commit a reversible error. At one point in the trial when Judge Wilbur Owens overruled one of Santa Lucia's numerous objections, Santa Lucia gave Scooter a nudge at the defendant's table.

I attended the trial every day, usually with my girlfriend at the time, who coincidentally lived next door to Judge Owens. At a cocktail party one evening, I found myself lighting Judge Owens's cigarette. I was told that he had asked my girlfriend's parents, a prominent retired army general and his lovely wife, why their daughter associated with "those people." I also flushed one day in court when a minor witness mentioned my name regarding an equally minor transaction involving Scooter and one gram of cocaine. The comment was not germane, as it had nothing to do with the charges against Scooter. Still, it was probably not an accident, and it alarmed me because I had no recollection of the transaction at the time.

After a short trial, the jury began their deliberations. They reached a quick verdict. I was driving back to court from lunch when I saw Buddy Yochim, Dickey's friend, on the courthouse steps giving me a signal—five fingers up, then a thumbs-down. Scooter had been convicted on all five counts and would be sentenced later.

Scooter had remained in jail the entire time. For strategic reasons, his attorneys thought it best he not make bail, and even though I tried my best to help with his legal expenses, I don't think we could have raised his bail quick enough; it was $100,000.00 cash. An immediate appeal of the verdict was planned, but Scooter would continue to remain in the Bibb County jail pending his sentencing. Albert Krieger from Miami, who later gained fame for representing the late John Gotti, would serve as Scooter's appeal attorney.

Macon was suddenly the place *not* to be. Gregg moved everything to Los Angeles to live with Cher and form a solo band. Dickey went back to Florida to start his own band. Butch moved to Tallahassee, and it would be a while before he performed again. Chuck, Lamar, and Jaimoe and guitarist Jimmy Nalls formed a group known as Sea Level. Later, Randall Bramblett, Davis Causey, and others were added. I was asked to be Sea Level's personal manager and immediately accepted. Chuck instructed me not to sign with Capricorn automatically, and we had discussions with Arista, Atlantic, and Warner Brothers. In the end, Capricorn gave us everything we asked for, and we signed a lucrative deal with them.

I was on the road with Sea Level when Scooter received a conditional sentence of fifteen years on each count for a total of seventy-five years. It was subject to further review after the Bureau of Prisons prepared a report on Scooter. The clear intimation to me was that they were still squeezing Scooter. It was made even clearer to him. Although the feds had pretty much given up hope of Scooter testifying on the other related offenses regarding so-called local organized crime, they told him he could help himself by informing against Phil Walden, Bunky Odom, or me. Scooter feigned interest, asking first for a conjugal visit from his wife Karen. Although highly irregular, his request was granted. After the visit, when the prosecutors appeared with a stenographer to take his statement, Scooter informed them that he wouldn't be able to help them after all. The feds went ballistic, saying he would serve the entire seventy-five years. One law enforcement official reportedly told Scooter that he didn't care if he lied or told the truth as long as he would swear to it. Scooter replied he would take his chances with his lawyers and his supporters. When I heard about this, I immediately retained two former federal prosecutors, now in private practice, to represent me. They reported that there was indeed interest in me at the federal prosecutor's office, but I was never charged and never heard another word about it. I believe to this day that part of this whole exercise had some connection with smearing Jimmy Carter's candidacy for president by indirectly linking him to a drug scandal.

Scooter was almost immediately transferred to the Atlanta Federal Penitentiary, one of the toughest joints in the federal penal system. Early on, he was going through the cafeteria line when he noticed a slight disturbance ahead of him. When he reached the spot, he saw an inmate on the floor bleeding from a knife wound. A voice behind him cautioned that he should act as if he saw nothing and keep moving. Also, early on, when asked about getting marijuana inside the prison, Scooter, perhaps foolishly, replied that he could. He quickly realized he would have to deliver or face dire consequences. Scott Hayes was hurriedly contacted, and feverish machinations began. I'm sure the Bureau of

Prisons would have been unhappy to learn that an inmate gardener found the requested pot under a bush on the grounds, right where it was supposed to be. This was clearly not the place for Scooter to be, and his wife grew more and more unhappy. I decided to find a way to get him out—soon.

Scooter's bail was $100,000.00 in cash plus related fees. With everyone's permission, except Gregg, who was not consulted, I went to Phil Walden with our predicament. He was able to get the band a royalty advance from Warner Bros. to cover the costs. A $100,000.00 bank certificate of deposit was transferred to the court. As I recall, the transaction was handled through Scooter's attorney by Mickey Shapiro of the Stuyvesant Bonding Company of Brooklyn, New York. Scooter was finally out on bail pending appeal of his conviction. Sea Level immediately hired him as their road manager.

Sea Level was a good band that highlighted the jazz influences of The Allman Brothers Band, and musically they were probably the best of the offshoot solo bands. Their albums sold well, though not in huge quantities, and their concert tours had early success. Gregg, Dickey, and Butch all tried the solo route, but the results were mostly disappointing. They had nothing new to offer. Gregg was anxious to get The Allman Brothers Band back together, and he met with Phil and Dickey and later with Butch. "Never again" became "maybe."

I was at work in my office when I heard the news that the U.S. Court of Appeals in New Orleans had overturned Scooter Herring's conviction. During his trial, the *Macon Telegraph* had published a front-page story regarding death threats made against Gregg Allman; it showed Gregg in the protective custody of U.S. marshals. At the time, Scooter's attorney had made a motion to poll the jury as to whether they had seen the story and if it might affect their verdict. Judge Owens denied the motion, and that's when Santa Lucia had given Scooter the high sign. Judge Owens now called in each juror for polling. I believe one was deceased, so the spouse was polled. When none of the jurors said they were prejudiced at the time of the trial, Judge Owens reinstated the seventy-five-year sentence. He was ultimately reversed again, and rather than face another trial with a similar verdict likely, Scooter pled guilty in August 1979 to one count of obtaining and possessing one gram of cocaine.

I wrote the most sincere and heartfelt letter I could to Judge Owens and begged for leniency, stressing Scooter's rehabilitation. Others did so as well. Judge Owens stated that he was impressed with what Scooter had done over the three-year period and, while not excusing him, set the sentence at only thirty months. The judge's remarks about Gregg were not so benevolent. Scooter's attorneys told him he would be imprisoned at a minimum-security facility at Eglin Air Force base in Florida, that two reputed organized crime inmates expected him there, and that he would have no problems. He served twelve months at Eglin, but after roughing up a snitch, he was transferred to a new facility in Talladega, Alabama, for an additional two months before spending sixty days at a halfway house back in Macon. Upon his final release, Scooter worked with Grinderswitch for a while, gravitating to tour bus driving for various bands. He ultimately ended up in management of video stores and auto parts stores. Scooter now resides in Alabama and has suffered from recent health problems. He and I remain in contact, and I will always admire him greatly.

Meanwhile, meetings were held about Chuck and Lamar joining an Allman Brothers Band reunion, but they also wanted to keep Sea Level together. When a full-time commitment was demanded, they opted out. Jaimoe had stopped touring with Sea Level because of recurring back problems, but he joined the reconstituted Allman Brothers Band. The new lineup included Gregg, Dickey, Jaimoe, and Butch, with Dan Toler on guitar and David Goldflies on bass. There was new personal management and many new lawyers, but the band's renegotiated recording contract stayed with Capricorn. The resultant album titled *Enlightened Rogues* was a vast improvement over *Win, Lose, or Draw*, but, again, trouble lay just ahead.

Capricorn Records, now distributed by Polygram Records, had lost money steadily. Cash advances from

Polygram financed them, and their own assets secured them. The Southern rock genre began to fall out of public favor, and an industry-wide sales recession occurred. Also, there was a huge arbitration award in favor of Dickey against Capricorn over prior royalties. Polygram pulled the plug and foreclosed. Later, Capricorn's phones were shut off, and we allowed their promotion department to use the phones at my management company and the Great Southern merchandising company. It was all to no avail, as Capricorn filed for bankruptcy and ceased normal day-to-day operations.

In November 1979, Twiggs Lyndon was killed when his parachute failed to open as he skydived in Duanesburg, New York. Many have speculated as to whether Twiggs took his own life, and I don't know the answer to that question. Since Twiggs was a meticulous veteran skydiver, it is inconceivable to me that he had a chute malfunction, but that is a remote possibility. Certainly, Twiggs had openly discussed suicide for years. As far back as the early sixties when I first met him, he outlined a detailed plan to crash an automobile into a police patrol car in Locust Grove, Georgia, a notorious speed trap near Macon, on his twenty-first birthday. On another occasion, he had attempted to jump headfirst from a speeding vehicle driven by Scott Hayes, declaring he wanted to die. I was able to grab him by his heels and hold on for dear life until the car stopped and we calmed him down.

As I prepared to leave my office in Macon to attend graveside services for Twiggs, I got an emergency call from Sea Level on the road. They were having a wintertime travel crisis somewhere in the midwest, and it required my immediate attention. Before his death, The Dixie Dregs, whom Twiggs managed, had recorded a song dedicated to him titled "Twiggs Approves." Twiggs would have enthusiastically approved my missing his funeral because of band business.

Sea Level's new unreleased album was a victim of Capricorn's demise, and soon Sea Level and I agreed to go our separate ways. They found new management and a new deal at Arista Records, but soon disbanded. Chuck, of course, went on to huge individual success with Eric Clapton and The Rolling Stones, and he is also a respected forester.

Later, we lost Lamar Williams to lung cancer. It has been widely speculated that he contracted the cancer from possible exposure to the defoliant Agent Orange while serving in Vietnam.

The Allman Brothers Band ended up at Arista as well, and the results there were mostly uninspired. They did have a minor hit single, "Straight from the Heart," but both Arista albums were critical and sales disappointments. Jaimoe sued the band in a financial dispute, and Dan Toler's brother Frankie replaced him. Gregg's heavy drinking was consistently getting him into trouble. He divorced Cher, remarried, and divorced again and had a child out of wedlock. After a performance on Saturday Night Live in 1982, the band broke up again.

I had been a stockholder in the Great Southern Company, and it had done well in the band merchandising business with a growing roster of famous clients. I went to work full-time there, but I couldn't get along with one of my partners, Ira Sokoloff. I sold my shares and spent most of my time for the next couple of years hanging out in bars, lying in the sun, and chasing the lovely local college co-eds. I was just past forty years of age and "at liberty," "between situations," and "available."

Duane Allman, Erie Raceway, Colorado, May 1971
©Steve Miles/courtesy Kirk West, ABB Archives

Berry Oakley at the Warehouse, New Orleans, 1971
©Sidney Smith/www.rockstarphotos.net

Butch Trucks, Macon, GA, April 1971   ©W. Robert Johnson,

Jaimoe at the annual Capricorn picnic, Macon, Ga, Summer 1974
© *Sidney Smith/www.rockstar photos.net*

Dickey Betts, New York State, Spring 1971   *Courtesy Kirk West/ABB Archives*

Gregg Allman, the Warehouse, New Orleans, New Year's Eve 1971
©Sidney Smith/www.rockstarphotos.net

John "Scooter" Herring and Gregg Allman, 1974
©Mark D. Paschall/courtesy of John "Scooter" Herring

Lamar Williams and Chuck Leavell at the farm, Juliette, GA, mid 1970's
©*Sidney Smith/www.rockstarphotos.net*

Rehearsal talk at the band warehouse, Macon, GA, 1973
©Gilbert Lee/www.gilbertlee.com,

Gregg Allman backstage at the Cow Palace, San Francisco, New Year's Eve, 1973-74
©Sidney Smith/www.rockstarphotos.net

The Gregg Allman Band (l-r) **Willie Perkins, Deryl Dawson, David "Frankie" Toler, Tim Heding, Bruce Waibel, Chaz Trippy, Gregg Voorhees; seated, John Emery, Gregg Allman, Dan Toler and Bud Snyder**   *©Kirk West*

29

I Get the Call Again

By early 1983, I'd had enough of "early retirement," so I decided to leave Macon. I rented out my house, moved in with Scott Hayes in Atlanta, and started testing the waters. My cash reserves were nearly gone, and I needed to start working again. Nevertheless, I leased a brand new, top-of-the-line Buick Park Avenue just to keep up appearances.

I first touched base with former Paragon Agency head Alex Hodges, who now ran his own booking agency in Atlanta. He had nothing for me at the time, but he later asked if I could work on retrieving a small amount of funds that had been frozen in an old Allman Brothers bank account in Macon. The money had been held in escrow for sales tax from a prior benefit concert. No tax liability was due, and Alex sought the funds for Gregg, whom he now represented. Alex and Gus Small, Gregg's divorce attorney, had formed a management company to try to resurrect Gregg's career. It was called, appropriately, Rescue Productions. Later, Gus opted out and a new company called Strike Force was formed. Using charm and diplomacy, I was able to convince the signatories on the bank account to release the funds on Gregg's behalf. Later, in November 1983, Gregg left me a phone message asking that I come back to work for him. I literally leapt for joy.

I drove to Jacksonville to see Gregg's band perform at a club called Playground South. I was shocked and saddened to see Gregg reduced to these circumstances, but he had a fine band anchored by the Toler brothers, Danny and Frankie, and his singing never sounded better. I immediately accepted the job to be his tour manager. Since I stopped working for him seven years earlier, Gregg had managed to get himself into terrible tax trouble, and the IRS had liens on much of his songwriting royalties. He had crippling child support and alimony payments and lived in a nice but small apartment in Sarasota. I believe he drove a used Pontiac Firebird. Financially and career-wise, he had nowhere to go but up. I bought a bumper sticker at a truck stop for Gregg's tour bus that read, "I Owe, I Owe, and off to Work I Go." Gregg was not amused, so I never put it on.

On our first road trip, we headed to the northeast. Between gigs in Washington, D.C., and Boston, we passed New York City, where we hadn't been able to arrange a gig. As we skirted the bright lights of the big city where we had some of our greatest triumphs, I silently swore that we would be back.

Things went fairly smoothly at first. I developed a pre-show routine with Gregg. I called him ninety minutes prior to leaving for the show to get him started. I called again thirty minutes later and again twenty minutes before departure time. Then I went to his room to escort him to the tour bus, gaining entry using my secret knock. Finally, I held my finger on the knot while Gregg tied his bandana around his forehead. He still required lots of attention, but our finances did not allow for a personal assistant at the time.

Gregg, like many entertainers, suffered from serious stage fright. Once he hit the first note, though, it disappeared. He often said he wanted to play every show like it was his last, and he usually did.

We played a steady circuit of clubs all over the country. In January 1984, Alex Hodges called me into his office and said things were moving fast. Strike Force had taken on Stevie Ray Vaughan as a client, and Alex decided to close his booking agency and take a position with ICM, the huge music, film, and literary agency in Los Angeles. Strike Force would now have offices in Atlanta and Los Angeles, and Alex offered me the position of handling the day-to-day activities of Gregg's management and overseeing the Atlanta office. I would also occasionally work out of Los Angeles and tour with Stevie Ray from time to time. The generous compensation would come on a percentage basis. If

Gregg prospered, so would I. Alex would retain the final word on any major career decisions involving Gregg. I gladly accepted the added responsibilities.

I still continued to travel with Gregg, as strict financial guidance was required in order for his tours to turn a profit. Economy with dignity was back in vogue again. There were no signs of drinking problems from Gregg, although cocaine use among Gregg, the band and crew, and myself was prevalent. Sometime around Memorial Day in 1984 at an outdoor show in Houston, the bus driver told me he found beer cans in the bathroom and thought Gregg had been drinking. He was right. Gregg had fallen off the wagon big time and became dreadfully sick. At Gregg's request, I immediately contacted his mother in Daytona Beach. I believe she had a prescription for lithium, which he thought would ease his discomfort. I sat up for hours that night helping Gregg through a violent illness, quite possibly alcohol poisoning. He threw up continuously in the trashcan at his bedside and was miserably sick throughout the entire night. The pills arrived the next day via overnight express, and the incident passed.

This was my first experience with the symptoms of acute alcoholism, and I was so frightened that I didn't take a drink for about a year afterward. As time went on, Gregg's setbacks with alcohol became much more frequent, and his periods of sobriety grew shorter. Gregg would usually volunteer to go in for periodic detox, but the drinking always returned more destructively each time. Gregg finally agreed to a twenty-eight-day treatment program in Nashville. Upon completion, he headed to his mother's place in Daytona. I met him as he changed planes in Atlanta, and he had gotten completely sloshed on the short flight from Nashville. I was crestfallen, and shortly thereafter I involved myself with Al-Anon—the program for friends, family, and employees of alcoholics—in order to help me understand and cope. I learned that no one can get a person suffering from the disease of alcoholism to stop drinking. It is completely up to the alcoholic. They must first admit they are powerless over alcohol and that their lives have become unmanageable. I can control my bad habits with sheer willpower, but an alcoholic cannot simply stop drinking by willpower alone. The process is much more complex. We did our best to provide conditions that were conducive to keeping Gregg sober. Ultimately, however, it was up to him.

There would be no meaningful comeback for Gregg without a record deal. He didn't have one, and the prospects for getting one were slim. His voice had never sounded better, and he had some decent material, but there was little interest. Gregg said all he wanted was to hear his music on the radio again. That really moved me, and I took another silent oath to help make it happen.

Alex Hodges had shopped Gregg's material to nearly every label, major and minor, when a friend suggested a song he had found by outside writers Tony

Colton and Phil Palmer. We all loved it because the lyrics sounded biographical, and the song had "hit" written all over it. Gregg and the band immediately cut a demo, and Alex ran it up the flagpole. Shortly thereafter, he got a call from Lenny Petze, an executive at Epic Records, an affiliate of CBS Records. As Alex recalls, Lenny had given a stack of demos to Bill Bennett, an independent radio consultant, to listen to on a flight from New York to Los Angeles. Bennett reported back to Petze that he could get Gregg's song on at least a hundred radio stations. The song was "I'm No Angel," and Epic was interested in making a deal.

I was ecstatic at the possibility of Gregg being back on a major label. We were in the northeast and drove our tour bus to CBS headquarters on West 52nd Street in Manhattan. I took Gregg up to meet with two of the A&R executives, Frank Rand and Michael Caplan. They came to a gig in New Jersey and gave a thumbs-up to Gregg and his band shortly thereafter. Later, Gregg, Frank Rand, and I flew to Los Angles to meet with the proposed producer, veteran Rodney Mills, best known for his work with Lynyrd Skynyrd and .38 Special. He and Gregg hit it off. Most of the elements were now in place, and Gregg soon signed a recording agreement. It was not a huge deal, but it was miles ahead of anything else on the horizon. We were back in the ballgame. Now all we had to do was deliver the album.

Rehearsals in Sarasota with Rodney Mills went well, and we quickly headed to Criteria Studios in Miami to begin recording. We rented the same house, as I recall, that Eric Clapton used when recording *461 Ocean Boulevard*. There was trouble the first night as Gregg fell off the wagon in a bad way and, when confronted, moved out to stay with a girlfriend. Soon he was back in the hospital for a dry out. Recording of the tracks went reasonably well, but when it came to the vocals, Gregg showed the effects of drinking. It was difficult for him to get satisfactory results for any length of time. Epic came close to pulling the plug on the entire project, which would have shattered Gregg's career. I can recall sitting up most of one night in the studio with Rodney Mills and Gregg's soundman and engineer, Bud Snyder, as they methodically took snippets of vocals from various takes to piece together completed tracks. They did a brilliant job. The results were seamless, and Epic was pleased with the final results.

The album *I'm No Angel* was released in early 1987. It was an immediate success, and the title track went to number-one on album-oriented radio stations, while the video was the ninth most popular on MTV for the year. The album subsequently earned a gold record award. Additional videos were filmed, and a second album was released and did almost as well, with additional number-one tracks on album radio. Bookings improved greatly, and we had a huge summer tour opening for Stevie Ray Vaughan and Double Trouble.

One working vacation took us to Hawaii, where we played three of the islands and had a few days off at a beautiful resort on Maui. There I met another of the great loves of my life, an adventurous free spirit named Sprite. We, too, have remained friends and keep in touch.

The Gregg Allman Band grossed more than a million dollars for the year from concerts alone, and Gregg slowly got back on his feet financially. The IRS liens were gone, and Gregg was current on all his obligations. An impending IRS audit was avoided using an entirely legal trick I had learned from a former IRS agent.

Gregg's battle with drugs and alcohol continued in periods of sobriety mixed with horrendous, nightmarish setbacks. I'd like to tip my hat to the Toler brothers and the rest of Gregg's band along with crew members Bud Snyder and John Emery and my office assistants Lisa Hernandez and Frieda Correll. They were behind Gregg 100 percent, and we couldn't have succeeded without them.

As the year 1989 approached, Alex, myself, and others started talking about a twentieth-anniversary reunion of The Allman Brothers Band. It wasn't exactly a stroke of genius, but we teased it well. Both of Gregg's solo albums had ended with live studio and actual live concert tracks of Allman Brothers songs. Epic Records had signed Dickey to a solo deal with thoughts of a reunion as well. We even booked Gregg's and Dickey's bands as a package, including an extended jam with both bands as an encore. It wasn't exactly The Allman

Brothers Band, but it was close. There were also a couple of low-key, unpublicized reunion benefit appearances, one at Charlie Daniels's Volunteer Jam and another for Bill Graham at Madison Square Garden.

I discovered that the trade name rights to "The Allman Brothers Band" had been allowed to expire. Alex Hodges and I went through the appropriate legal procedures to acquire the rights for Gregg. We seriously considered cutting ourselves in for a percentage of ownership based on our discovery of the oversight and our action on behalf of Gregg, but ultimately we decided against it on ethical grounds. That probably cost Alex and me hundreds of thousands of dollars in uncollected usage fees.

Things were not uneventful on tour with The Gregg Allman Band either. In Hattiesburg, Mississippi, we had yet another drug bust, again with suspicious overtones of it being a setup. My roommate had a small amount of marijuana, and we both learned that we were under arrest. Subsequently, the officers told us we were not to be charged and were free to go. They were obviously looking for something else. A guest at the previous evening's show had provided heavy-duty party favors, and we now suspected he was an informant. The search was not over, but I was free to move about, so, surreptitiously, I headed for an out-of-the-way room occupied by the road crew. After gaining entry from a slowly awakening roadie, I excitedly asked if they had any coke. The still sleepy reply was "Yeah, there's a pile on the nightstand. Help yourself." That was not the answer I wanted, and I quickly disposed of the contraband. Once again, the search was haphazard; no one was charged and we went on our way.

Not amusing at all was my last brush with a Gregg Allman overdose. We were on tour with Stevie Ray Vaughan and had experienced a hugely successful show at The Pier overlooking the Hudson River in New York City. We were just about to check out of the Mayflower Hotel near Central Park on the morning afterward when I got an emergency call to come to Gregg's room. He had overdosed on a depressant and was not breathing. Efforts to revive him did not go well, and he started turning blue; luckily, though, the paramedics I had called arrived quickly and revived him. I sent the band to that night's show in the tour bus and accompanied Gregg to the hospital. Later that day, I hastily arranged a flight for the two of us, and we arrived at the outdoor venue moments before show time as if nothing extraordinary had happened. It was a close call for the show and an even closer call for Gregg.

After various meetings, we reached agreement for a twentieth-anniversary reunion of The Allman Brothers Band with Gregg, Dickey, Butch, and Jaimoe. The new sidemen were Warren Haynes, Allen Woody, and, temporarily, Johnny Neel. Alex Hodges and I managed

Gregg through his Strike Force company, while Danny Goldberg, a highly successful personal manager and later label head, managed Dickey, Butch, and Jaimoe. Danny was and is a great person, but a natural rivalry existed between Alex and Danny, and relations were often bumpy. A summer tour was planned to coincide with Polygram's release of the retrospective box set *Dreams*, for which Alex and I received executive producer credits. A new studio album on Epic was to follow. The tour did respectable business and the future looked bright.

The future was not bright for Strike Force, though. On the last day of the contract renewal period with Gregg, I was with him looking at a house he wanted to buy in Nashville. I didn't hear a peep from Gregg about it, but his attorney faxed our office in Atlanta at the last possible minute with the news that Gregg was exercising his option not to renew his management agreement with Strike Force. I had worked thirteen of the previous twenty years for and with Gregg. I had helped him financially and personally over and over again. I had saved him from the law, saved him from the IRS, and, on several occasions, helped save his life, and I was paid well for it. Money aside, I loved Gregg Allman, warts and all, and my heart was broken. I would have appreciated at least a thank-you and good-bye. I got neither.

30

A Few Words about Finances

Much has been said and written over the years about the finances of The Allman Brothers Band, mostly by people who had no idea what they were talking about. To be blunt, I never stole a penny from the band and have seen no compelling evidence that Phil Walden or any of his companies did either.

Phil Walden was a tough, hard-nosed businessman, but his business agreements hardly differed from those of most managers, agents, or record labels of that era. Some would say he had an inherent conflict of interest because of his role as both personal manager and record label head, and on the surface, that's a valid point, but it was not uncommon at the time. Certainly, there would have been no Allman Brothers Band without him. Early on, all the major New York booking agents said you couldn't succeed with a band that included two drummers, two guitarists, and a lead singer sitting behind an organ. Phil stood up for the band, and the agents were proved wrong.

Without Phil Walden, there possibly wouldn't even have been a first album, much less a follow-up to that slow-selling record. Certainly, it's unlikely that there would have been a live, double, specially-priced third album. Also, Phil had advanced the band around $150,000.00, a huge sum at the time, before there was any indication that they would earn enough to pay him back. Finally, the band was brilliantly packaged and booked in a way that maximized their personal appearance income potential.

The band members never paid management commissions on their recording, writing, or publishing royalties and paid for no studio recording or rehearsal time at Capricorn Studios in Macon. In addition, Phil Walden was contractually entitled to reimbursement of expenses when traveling on behalf of the band. I don't recall him charging back any of his travel, although we might have picked up Bunky Odom's travel expenses periodically. Phil and I also encouraged the band to make wise investments, although that advice fell mostly on deaf ears. I'm certainly not a shill for Phil Walden, but he deserves a fair shake in any discussion of the band's finances.

As far as recording audits go, the auditor is expected to show that the company owes the artist huge sums, while the company's accountants and lawyers can look at the same data and show that the artist owes the company. The correct answer is usually somewhere in the middle. I was always somewhat mystified that the attorneys the band members hired never went after the original distributors, Atlantic and Warner Brothers. They were the entities that computed royalties and issued the checks. It wasn't until the last album under the Polygram agreement that the band received recording royalties directly from Capricorn. One should always check the party that touches the money first, regardless of the enterprise. Was there perhaps an ulterior motive by the attorneys and new management to make Phil Walden the villain?

Afterword

After the tragic accidental death of Stevie Ray Vaughan, Alex Hodges shut down Strike Force. Today, he is a successful executive with the House of Blues concert promotion company. Phil Walden revived Capricorn Records, and it was hugely successful again. He recently sold the new masters but retained the name. He is currently working on a feature film project and a possible relaunching of the Capricorn label and studio.

The Allman Brothers Band has been inducted into the Rock and Roll Hall of Fame. They remain one of the evergreen acts of rock as they perform a hugely popular series of concerts every year at the Beacon Theater in New York and at the outdoor sheds in the summer. However, many of their fans were shocked and saddened at the firing of Dickey Betts several years back. Dickey continues to perform as a solo artist along with his band Great Southern, featuring Dan Toler. A year or so after firing Dickey, the band called for the forced "early retirement" of Red Dog, a roadie who served them for more than thirty years and who had achieved almost icon status. This further alienated some of the longtime fans.

Untimely death would continue to plague The Allman Brothers Band family when road crew member Joe Dan Petty perished in a private plane accident in

Macon. Also, bassist Allen Woody passed away shortly thereafter.

I went to one of the band's concerts a couple of years ago and witnessed a lineup featuring Warren Haynes, Derek Trucks, Oteil Burbridge, and Marc Quinones. My friend Elizabeth and I were given VIP seats on the stage and treated cordially. Butch and Jaimoe, manager Bert Holman, and tour manager Kirk West warmly greeted me. When I met briefly with Gregg afterward, all he could say was "Can you believe I actually survived?" I understand that he has enjoyed several good years of sobriety, and I am relieved and happy that he is now able to take joy in his music and his family.

I wish them all well.

After Strike Force shut down, I opened my own company, Republic Artists Management, and even put together a short southern tour for The Gregg Allman Band and helped Scott Hayes promote successful solo dates for Gregg in Atlanta. I also formed a small independent record label, Atlas Records, and moved my operations back to Macon. I work with some amazingly talented blues/rock veterans, Sonny Moorman and Mike Reilly, as well as with a budding teen talent, Tony Tyler, who has a potentially great career ahead of him. Check them out.

Personally, I take great pleasure in the serenity of Macon, with my home surrounded by tall Georgia pines, and I enjoy my hobby of collecting and working on old cars. I treasure the company of a few longtime close friends, the love of my family, and the love of my dear friend Elizabeth. Life would probably have been pretty ordinary had I not experienced my adventures with The Allman Brothers Band.

Life is short. Break some rules. Have some fun.

Macon, Georgia
August 2004

"I love being alive and I will be the best man I possibly can. I will take love wherever I find it and offer it to whoever will take it … seek knowledge from those wiser … and teach those who wish to learn from me."

—*Duane Allman's epitaph from his journal*

Duane Allman   *Courtesy Kirk West/ABB Archives*

Index